BLUEPRINT FOR AMERICA

BLUEPRINT FOR AMERICA

EDITED BY

George P. Shultz

CONTRIBUTING AUTHORS

Scott W. Atlas • Michael J. Boskin

John H. Cochrane • John F. Cogan

James O. Ellis Jr. • James E. Goodby

Eric A. Hanushek • James N. Mattis

Kori Schake • George P. Shultz

John B. Taylor

HOOVER INSTITUTION PRESS

Stanford University | Stanford, California

*With its eminent scholars and world-renowned library
and archives, the Hoover Institution seeks to improve the
human condition by advancing ideas that promote economic
opportunity and prosperity, while securing and safeguarding
peace for America and all mankind. The views expressed in its publications
are entirely those of the authors and do not necessarily reflect the views of
the staff, officers, or Board of Overseers of the Hoover Institution.*

www.hoover.org

Hoover Institution Press Publication No. 673
Hoover Institution at Leland Stanford Junior University,
Stanford, California 94305-6003

First printing 2016
22 21 20 19 18 17 16   9 8 7 6 5 4 3 2 1

Manufactured in the United States of America

The paper used in this publication meets the minimum requirements of the
American National Standard for Information Sciences—Permanence of Paper
for Printed Library Materials, ANSI/NISO Z39.48-1992. ♾

Library of Congress Cataloging-in-Publication Data
Names: Shultz, George Pratt, 1920– editor.
Title: Blueprint for America / edited by George P. Shultz.
Other titles: Hoover Institution Press publication ; 673.
Description: Stanford, CA : Hoover Institution Press, 2016. | Series: Hoover
   Institution Press publication ; no. 673 | Includes bibliographical
   references and index.
Identifiers: LCCN 2016029379 | ISBN 9780817919955 (pbk. : alk. paper) |
   ISBN 9780817919962 (EPUB) | ISBN 9780817919979 (Mobipocket) |
   ISBN 9780817919986 (EPDF)
Subjects: LCSH: United States—Politics and government—21st century. |
   United States—Economic policy. | National security—United States. |
   United States—Foreign relations—21st century.
Classification: LCC E893 .B58 2016 | DDC 320.60973—dc23
LC record available at https://lccn.loc.gov/2016029379

CONTENTS

ACKNOWLEDGMENTS

In their 1972 political economy treatise on the Garbage Can Theory of complex organizational decision-making, Michael Cohen, James March, and Johan Olsen used the example of the American university to describe a fraught nature whereby "active decision-makers and problems track one another through a series of choices without appreciable progress in solving problems." It is an apt model.

In that light, we would like to recognize our colleagues at the Hoover Institution for their help keeping the authors' efforts on time and on track—and this *Blueprint* out of the garbage can: Tunku Varadarajan, Susan Schendel, and David Fedor, along with Chris Dauer and Barbara Arellano's team at Hoover Press.

George P. Shultz was the impetus and is the continued driving force for this *Blueprint*. His counsel and friendship—and a lucid optimism toward American faculties—are an inspiration.

The Authors
HOOVER INSTITUTION
Stanford University

INTRODUCTION

Although the word "blueprint" originally referred to a detailed architectural or mechanical plan, it has grown to acquire a more metaphorical meaning. We have chosen the word deliberately because it conveys our intent to offer a coherent set of ideas for the rebuilding of America. This book offers a plan for civic, economic, and security architecture in the broadest sense, for the construction of a solvent America that this generation can bequeath without guilt to the next.

America has long offered a political and economic example to the rest of the world. From its earliest days, its political principles have been rooted in universality, not narrow nationalism; and over the years, it has thrown its doors open to people from every corner of the globe. There is a reason why America draws immigrants not only from lands that are poorer and less well-governed than our own, but also from places where people fare well.

But this American ability to inspire—which we call Exceptionalism—is not automatic. It takes continued efforts to be realized in a changing world. We face challenges today. Washington is rent along partisan lines, seemingly unwilling to work toward useful compromise. This ideological partisanship is compounded by demographic changes that are prone to exploitation by populists on the left and right. A deep recession and an anemic recovery have shaken widespread faith in policies and principles that have served this country admirably for generations.

Add to this threats to global order, from newly emergent nationalistic state assertiveness to the galloping threat of Islamist extremism. The meltdown in the Middle East—particularly in Syria and Iraq—has also had a profoundly destabilizing impact on Europe, shaking some of our closest allies to the core and underlining the need for American global engagement.

Our *Blueprint* offers a series of policy ideas that would help shore up the long-term foundations of American strengths. This book has assembled a series of essays, both explanatory and prescriptive, written by scholars at the Hoover Institution—all professors, thinkers, and practitioners of global renown in their respective fields:

✓ Economic success offers the key to America's continued primacy in virtually every global field. It is no accident that our perceived receding from the world's stage has occurred over a prolonged period of sluggish growth, at a rate barely above stagnation. So that is where we start. The economists Michael Boskin, John Cogan, John Cochrane, and John Taylor—a formidable quartet by any standard—address the questions of entitlement reform, deficits, monetary reform, national debt, and regulatory and tax reform.

✓ Health care has become such a large part of our economy that it deserves it own discussion: Scott Atlas draws on his front-line tours in the practice of medicine to tackle health care reform and the problems generated by the Affordable Care Act.

✓ The *Blueprint*'s focus then shifts toward the inputs of our nation's global competitiveness. Cochrane returns to reframe the discourse on immigration and international trade. Eric Hanushek meanwhile addresses the reform of K-12 education, a sphere in which this country lags dangerously behind its competitors, even as its universities continue to set the highest standards.

✓ Rounding off the international dimension of our *Blueprint* are essays by retired admiral James Ellis, retired general James Mattis, and Kori Schake on their vision of how to restore America's national security. Ellis follows that with a deep-dive on our (sorely lacking) energy security strategy, and James Goodby expounds on the country's practice of diplomacy in a time of turbulent transition.

Across all of this, our project "foreman" George Shultz draws from his own experiences in government, industry, and academia to lead off each section with a range of observations—some prescriptive, others reflective—on spending, human resources, foreign policy, and, in conclusion, the art of governance.

This is not a book of empty rhetoric; nor is it one of ideologically skewed or partisan censure. Yes, there is criticism offered and blame ascribed; but they are directed at the bad ideas and policies that have hamstrung America and knocked it off course. The spirit of our *Blueprint* is wholly positive: we offer ideas, diagnoses, solutions, and road maps. There is a lot of work that can yet be done, so let's get started.

BLUEPRINT FOR AMERICA

CHAPTER 1

THE DOMESTIC LANDSCAPE

Michael J. Boskin

A merica is at a historic crossroads. Two in three citizens believe the country is on the wrong track, a majority that the next generation will be worse off than this one.

The next president and Congress face domestic crises that must be addressed robustly if our country is to enjoy widely distributed prosperity. Those taking office need strategies and ideas to deal with the issues and they must recruit the best talent to use their offices effectively. We set out here a *Blueprint for America* in an effort to define these issues. The first part of this book deals with the domestic economic spheres.

Too much contemporary policy discussion has focused on short-run issues while neglecting the long. The 2008–09 recession led to an obsessive debate on how to deal with the present downturn. As difficult as this economic condition has been, it is modest relative to the issues of long-run growth; and it is that growth which will determine the well-being of Americans and their position in the world.

THE ECONOMY

A strong economy means long-term prosperity for Americans. So economic policies are the critical foundation for raising living standards, growing government revenue for necessary national purposes, and reducing social conflict over the division of the pie.

Through all the vicissitudes from World War II to the Great Recession, the American economy averaged more than 3 percent annual growth. Yet it has not had as few as three consecutive quarters of 3-percent growth in a decade. Recoveries from other deep post-war recessions averaged growth of 4 percent or more for several years. Yet the recovery from the 2008–09 recession has averaged just over 2 percent. So among our economic and social priorities, the strongest possible economic growth comes first.

The case for growth is not hard to make, but that doesn't mean we shouldn't make it. Economic growth is determined by gains in productivity and the growth in the number of workers. Government economic policies—fiscal, monetary, regulatory, and trade—must be designed to support the strongest possible non-inflationary growth. Productivity gains, which determine wage increases, are driven by improved technology and investment in capital and worker skills.

To encourage growth and associated improvements in living standards, the private sector must have incentives for innovation, entrepreneurship, and investment in physical and human capital. We must cut red tape, rein in deficits and debt, enact tax policies conducive to capital formation and work, reform the education system, and invest in precompetitive generic research and development. These specific policies must be embedded in sound macroeconomic monetary and fiscal policy that lays a foundation for economic growth.

THE SIZE AND SCOPE OF GOVERNMENT

A successful society needs an effective government. There are important functions for which the federal, state, or local government has a natural comparative advantage and which should not be left to private markets. It is essential that government perform these functions effectively and that its revenues are adequate to fund its necessary functions.

Examples of successful government programs include the military that has kept us free for almost 240 years; the GI Bill that was an investment in human capital; and a Social Security system that has reduced poverty among the elderly. Even successful programs, however, can be implemented at lower cost, and more effectively. Social Security was designed, in the words of President Franklin Roosevelt, "to secure a measure of protection against poverty-ridden old age." Yet someone earning the Social Security maximum taxable earnings will retire with Social Security benefits of more than twice the poverty level, not counting any other sources of income. Does that make sense?

Just as markets sometimes fail, there are government failures. These include crony capitalism, rent-seeking (i.e., using the political system to obtain special economic gains), regulatory capture, excessive social engineering, incompetence, waste, and corruption. Recent examples include three million phony tax refunds paid by the IRS, a 21 percent fraud rate in the earned income tax credit, massive fraud in Medicare and Medicaid, billions in unpaid income tax, and the "capture" of bank regulators that contributed to the financial crisis.

To be sure, even the most successful private enterprises sometimes fail. Apple flopped with the Lisa and the Newton. But that didn't hinder great success, given the willingness to recognize those failures and try a different approach. While market forces weed out the failures, there is no mechanism to eliminate failed government programs. When government becomes so large that it performs unnecessary functions—and necessary ones abjectly—reform is essential. A major reexamination is overdue, one designed to make the government more effective at serving citizens at lower cost to taxpayers.

The General Accountability Office identified 162 areas where federal programs overlap or fragment. For example, the federal government has ninety-two programs designed to help low-income Americans, costing over $800 billion per year. Do we really need forty-six job-training programs, sprawling over nine

agencies, costing $20 billion a year, many with no metrics . . .
seventeen federal food-aid programs across three agencies costing
$100 billion per year . . . and twenty federal housing programs
across three departments costing $50 billion a year?

The cumulative effect of this proliferation of programs can
be pernicious. The Congressional Budget Office (CBO) reports
that the interaction of several anti-poverty programs leaves some
low-income Americans with marginal tax rates approaching 100
percent. How? The benefits phase out as income rises (to avoid
supporting people further up the income distribution). But when
several programs start to phase out simultaneously, a low-income
worker may face the prospect of working more, but with any additional income offset by an equal reduction in benefits phased
out. In short, a massive work disincentive traps them in continu-
ous dependency. The time is due for an aggressive modernization
and consolidation of programs and the elimination of those that
burn the taxpayers' investment.

SPENDING

Government spending has gotten out of control, and with it our
national debt. Low interest rates have helped to drop the issue off
of the political radar, but they will not last. Studies suggest that
slowing spending growth enough to prevent projected large increases in the national debt, as a share of gross domestic product,
would increase GDP by 15 percent or more in a generation. Doing this, while preserving the already declining proportions of our
budget reserved for basic government functions such as defense
and infrastructure, will absolutely require entitlement reform. For
Social Security, that means, at the basic level, a change from wage-
to price-indexing in calculating initial benefits. It is a good job
for Washington politicians to figure out the tactical maneuvers
required to do so.

Federal research and development (R&D) spending is short-
term and sometimes degenerates into an industrial policy of
picking commercial winners and losers. Policies to encourage

innovation in the private sector as well as more, and more effective, R&D funding from the federal government are essential to strong economic growth.

IN HEALTH CARE, improvements are more complex. Demographics are changing as the population ages. The incidence of the most disabling diseases, including some that require expensive technology and drugs for diagnosis and treatment, will rise. Obesity, a most serious public health problem, assures unprecedented costs and harm. The nation's fiscal challenges will likely worsen in the absence of change. Medicaid and Medicare have expanded to consume over a trillion dollars per year, while physician acceptance of patients under those programs has continued to diminish. National health expenditures are again projected significantly to outpace GDP.

Yet the twenty-first century holds vivid promise for medical care. We are entering a new era in which genetics, medical technology, and new drugs will change medicine to a more personalized system of earlier diagnoses, targeted treatments, and prevention. To fix the inadequacies and reduce the cost of American health care without jeopardizing its excellence, significant reforms are essential.

The best way to control prices is through competition for empowered, value-seeking consumers. The key is to replace centralized models based on misguided incentives to one of individual empowerment with personal responsibility. Refocus the system toward one of bottom-up control, with incentives for high-deductible catastrophic insurance coverage and health savings accounts (HSAs) for better value and more consumer choices across services of known prices.

TAX REFORM

The primary purpose of taxation should be to raise the revenue necessary to finance government spending. While governments may also borrow, debt must be repaid or refinanced, and in either case will require higher future taxes. Federal spending is projected to grow rapidly, the primary drivers being the costs of entitlements and higher interest costs on the growing debt. In order to cover the cost of projected spending in, say, 2040, income and/or payroll tax rates would have to rise so much that middle-income families could face marginal tax rates over 60 percent. That is a recipe for permanent stagnation.

Taxes distort economic decisions. By reducing after-tax wages and returns to saving, income tax reduces work and saving. The corporate income tax discourages capital formation, encourages excessive leverage, and reallocates capital by industry and sector with its numerous special provisions. These biases ensure that overall capital formation runs steeply uphill, with deleterious consequences.

The harm from these distortions rises with the square of the tax rate, so doubling the rate quadruples the harm. This is the primary reason to keep marginal tax rates as low as possible while raising sufficient revenue to fund the necessary functions of government. Tax systems with low rates and broad bases are the most effective foundation for an efficient, growing economy. Replacing the current personal and corporate income taxes with a broad-based, low-rates tax on consumed income could increase GDP by 6–15 percent. Studies of the tax base conclude that the corporate tax is the most harmful to growth, followed by income taxes, with taxes on consumption the least harmful.

The United States has the highest corporate tax rate among the leading economies, thereby encouraging companies to operate elsewhere. Our statutory rate is 35 percent, compared with Canada at 15 percent, Germany at 15.8 percent, Japan at 24 percent, or the United Kingdom at 20 percent. We also tax again on any corporate earnings that are repatriated, even though they were already taxed in the country where they were earned. The result: an estimated $2 trillion that we need for investment and hiring remains abroad.

To avoid holding the economy back, we must get the corporate rate at least in line with the 25 percent average rate in other OECD (Organisation for Economic Co-operation and Development) countries and end the double taxation of earnings so that money can be repatriated and invested and spent here.

REGULATION

Government regulation is pervasive. While designed to achieve social benefits like reduced pollution, it also imposes a substantial cost—a de facto tax—on businesses and households. While most of our laws and Supreme Court rulings wisely demand a balancing of benefits and costs, studies estimate the annual cost of regulation at well over a trillion dollars.

Even scaling down the estimates of costs and taking a generous view of benefits leaves an opportunity for huge economic gains from improvement in the regulatory apparatus. Far more rigorous implementation of unbiased cost-benefit analyses is needed. An overall regulatory budget cap and the requirement that an old regulation of comparable cost be removed for every new regulation imposed—as in Canada—are also options.

To be sure, there may be health, safety, environmental, or other benefits to justify many regulations, and some sectors need regulation. For most of the previous century, economic regulation of "natural" monopolies, e.g., utilities in telecommunications, electricity, and transportation, dominated the regulatory terrain. With large fixed costs, demand was insufficient to support more than one or a very few firms. To gain some of the benefits of competition and decrease monopoly or oligopoly pricing, regulatory commissions set prices sufficient to earn a reasonable return for the firm. Insufficient incentive was left to innovate, as firms had little upside.

But in some cases, regulators are captured by the very industry they regulate. The banking regulators were asleep at the wheel in the path to the financial crisis of 2008–09. As technology has become vitally important in the economy, the notion of Schumpe-terian creative destruction has reemerged. In short, monopoly and monopoly profits eventually beget new technology, competitors, and platforms that undermine the entrenched monopoly and give way to a new one. Thus serial monopoly may be good for innova-tion and less harmful to consumers than traditionally argued, at least if the new firms come along at a rapid enough pace.

Of course, much regulation was not of "natural" monopolies, but of unnatural ones created by government through regulation and licensing that foreclosed entry of new firms. An important current upheaval is the competition Uber is providing to regu-lated taxis. There are many such real-world examples where lifting regulatory restrictions substantially lowered prices and spurred in-novation in telecommunications, trucking, airlines, and package delivery. Such successes should make us think twice about a new wave of regulation.

Our regulatory system presents companies with a maze of ab-struse requirements. The result is onerous compliance costs for large companies and discouragement to smaller companies that cannot afford compliance expenses.

FINANCIAL REGULATION

The basic structure of financial regulation has failed. In that struc-ture, the government guarantees debts through deposit insurance and bailouts, in order to stop runs. To offset the consequent in-centives to take on too much risk with government-guaranteed funding, the government tries to regulate banks' and financial institutions' investment decisions. But over and over, the regula-tors fail to stop excessive leverage, a panic ensues, and the gov-ernment bails out a wider set of investors. We must escape this treadmill.

The answer is capital. Banks and other financial institutions that hold risky assets must get their money primarily by issu-ing stock or long-term debt or by retaining earnings. An equity-financed bank literally cannot fail. It has made no promises that can land it in bankruptcy court. It cannot suffer a run. This extreme is not necessary for our financial system, but it makes clear just how effective an equity-financed financial system could be to eliminate bankruptcies with no bailouts and no regulation.

The government should first remove distortions, subsidies, and regulatory incentives that currently favor too much debt. Debt, and especially short-term debt, is the poison in the well that causes financial crises.

For example, interest payments are tax-deductible; dividend payments are not. They should at least be treated equally. Debt is favored as an asset by capital and liquidity regulation, which gives an incentive to produce too much of it. Asset and liquidity regulation should focus on getting through a crisis without selling and running, not encouraging individual firms to hold liquid short-term debt on which they can quickly run. Capital-gains taxation makes it hard to use floating-value assets for transactions, though they may be perfectly liquid. And the multiple subsidies for consumer, housing, student loan, and corporate debt should be gradually phased out.

Second, there should be a regulatory safe harbor for equity-financed firms. If a firm is funded more than half by equity and less than 10 percent by short-term debt, for example, then the vast apparatus of asset regulation no longer applies. Banks that complain of current regulation will then voluntarily capitalize. Unlike current regulation, there must be a definition of how a company can organize itself so as not to cause a systemic threat and a safe harbor from regulation for companies that comply.

FINALLY, when regulations are needed, the best ones are visible and easy to enforce. The maze of the Dodd-Frank Act could be replaced by two simple measures: capital requirements that rise in percentage terms with the size of the financial institution involved and reasonable restrictions on the use of leverage. We also need to position the Treasury Department and the Federal Reserve Board to make it clear that they will protect the financial system—not individual financial institutions. If an organization is mismanaged, let it fail.

MONETARY POLICY

Monetary policy is key to a healthy, noninflationary economy, but there is often uncertainty about what the Fed will do. Federal Reserve governors have different opinions, and they sound off. The great Red Sox slugger, Ted Williams, handled complaints that he didn't talk enough by saying, "I let my bat do the talking." The Fed carries a big bat, which it does not always use wisely.

The long period of very low interest rates has obscured the burden of the large debt that has piled up. It has also produced unprecedented assets now in the hands of the Fed, which must be returned to the market. A credible renormalization of interest rates and a gradual reduction in the size of the Fed's balance sheet are essential to removing distortions and creating the conditions for strong economic growth.

A great deal of uncertainty in the international monetary system is due to these unconventional monetary policies, including large-scale asset purchases, which buffet around and distort exchange rates. A more strategic rules-based monetary policy will remove these distortions.

INTERNATIONAL TRADE

Open, rules-based international trade has been a bipartisan foundation of American economic policy since World War II. Protectionist policies contributed to the Great Depression; successive rounds of negotiations to reduce barriers to trade helped propel the mostly good times in the post–World War II decades. Contrary to what some are saying, NAFTA (the North American Free Trade Agreement) has been of great benefit to the United States, Canada, and Mexico; has built cohesion in the continent; and, evidence shows, boosted real wages and societal welfare in each country.

With trade promotion authority, the president has the essential authority to negotiate trade agreements, with Congress having an up-or-down vote without amendments to the agreement. In addition to the Trans Pacific Partnership awaiting action, additional agreement should be explored as opportunities allow.

Recently, there has been an uptick in objections to free trade agreements based on trade deficits or "unfair" exchange rates, but these are largely unfounded: trade deficits occur when saving is too low relative to investment; exchange rate swings are often due to discretionary monetary-policy reactions in different countries. On both counts, the best medicine is in improving incentives to save and a steadier rules-based monetary policy—not protectionism. Trade adjustment assistance must also be improved.

HUMAN RESOURCES

Rounding out our domestic economic policy priorities is the recognition that growth derives from our national human resources: an expansion in, and an increase in the productivity of, the labor force. But today's population is aging rapidly, and labor force participation rates are also dropping; the prime labor force is not increasing. Education and immigration both have a role to play here.

The United States has a skills renewal problem that has direct implications for economic growth, individual well-being, and income distribution. Employers list millions of unfilled jobs, saying they cannot find workers with even basic skills, and US students lag behind achievement levels of many countries. If skills could be lifted through better schooling, and reinforced by more successful job training, GDP would increase by an estimated 6 percent or more. Improving schools requires commitment, and the key is to raise teacher quality: evidence shows that strong accountability, direct financial rewards for superior teachers, dismissal of ineffective teachers, and greater parental choice of schools all contribute to better performance.

Meanwhile, as the population ages and the ratio of workers–to–retirees falls, it will be increasingly important to keep able people in the labor force longer. Policy changes can help—changes to the payroll tax for older workers, for example, that would incentivize both employer and employee to keep working. At the same time, both demographics and education underscore the importance of changing our immigration system so that greater emphasis is put on the potential productivity of those who come to America, as in virtually every other developed country—with a particular emphasis on bringing in, or simply retaining, educated people of working age.

It is important to fight the right battles. Mexico, with fertility rates that are falling to below the replacement level and an improving economy, is no longer the leading source of immigrants to the United States, legal or otherwise. Immigration reform needs to move beyond just "securing our borders" and recognize that the bigger goal is to work with Mexico to prevent it becoming a migrant transit country as we are challenged to renew our nation's own highly skilled and productive work force.

The nation must also find a way to deal with undocumented workers and families already here. It is contrary to our heritage to consign those who have lived and worked here to a different class. As we reform immigration policies, we should develop paths to eventual citizenship for those already here who meet sensible criteria.

In sum, the needs are obvious, and we can meet them if we strengthen growth, which will pull people back into the labor force; offer choice, competition, and accountability in K-12 education to increase achievement; enact reforms that help people remain productive in their senior years; and reform immigration to encourage the flow of the brightest to our shores.

ECONOMIC POLICY MUST BE DEBATED in every genera-
tion, because the principles become hostage to the short-term political purposes of various interests. Good economic policy rests
on timeless principles. We've got cleaning up to do. No set of
policies can eliminate all risks or banish all economic problems.
But we are confident that the policies described here are intellec-
tually sound and historically successful and will provide the foundation for economic progress and rising standards of living for all
Americans.

SPENDING

George P. Shultz

I have a history in the construction industry. Given that this book is billed as a policy "blueprint," it's an appropriate background. An important part of any construction site is the supervisor's morning briefing: an overview of the day's work agenda and identification of important issues to be resolved in the field. So let me try that approach here, too.

Across all the domestic issues that our government should be paying attention to, the unsustainable path of our public expenditures is probably the most important. Before my Hoover colleagues weigh in on other details, then, I want to start by emphasizing this theme and a few basic priorities.

We must get control of spending in the United States. Here's why. A huge federal debt has been piled up in reaction to the Great Recession. The burden of that debt has been obscured by the sustained low interest rate policy by the Federal Reserve Board. Once interest rates return to normal levels, the burden of the debt will skyrocket, easily coming to 20 percent of current budget levels.

Projections of other spending by the Congressional Budget Office show that control of spending means facing up to the almost certain rise in the proportion of the budget spent on entitlements.

These automatic spending prospects mean that the basic functions of government tend to be crowded out of adequate funding. For example, funding for defense is now at a low and inadequate level. Our basic infrastructure is in need of extensive work to bring it to levels that are safe, functionally adequate, and visually appealing.

Social Security is relatively easy to deal with conceptually, but the politics of the issue are always difficult. What needs to be done, for those sixty years of age and younger, is to change from wage-indexing to price-indexing in calculating benefits. And as the age of full benefits rises from sixty-five to sixty-seven, index that age to changes in longevity. Price-indexing means that younger workers would have the system saved for them and would get today's level of benefits protected from inflation.

The last time the Social Security system was brought back into balance was 1983, as part of the political magic worked by Speaker of the House Tip O'Neill and President Reagan. Congress created a commission, with the general understanding that the recommendations of the commission would go into effect unless the package were voted down by the House or Senate. So constructive changes were made by the so-called Greenspan Commission and nobody had to vote for them. Call it a cop-out, if you will, but it was a salient nuance that worked.

Health care is much more complicated and more difficult, but there may very well be shaping up a way to get at this issue. Preventive medicine is becoming more and more important, bringing with it improved quality of lives and reductions in cost. An ounce of prevention is worth a pound of cure—maybe many pounds. In addition, prevention tends to make individuals much more conscious of their health needs and requirements. We very well may see a gradual shift in the system from the top-down prescriptive mandated system to one that is more responsive to bottom-up control with competition and known prices and outcomes.

HEALTH SAVINGS ACCOUNTS (HSAs) are the vehicle for putting more control in the hands of individuals. The use of these accounts is already rising significantly, having grown to cover 17 million people over the past decade. Now almost one-third of all employers offer some type of health savings account and HSA deposits have reached $24 billion. Medicare and Medicaid can be changed to allow adequate HSAs to be provided to those eligible for these programs. Together, these actions amount to making access to health care systems universally available.

This system will also benefit when predictable, ordinary medical expenses are paid out of HSAs as distinct from the present method of having insurance cover close to everything. Insurance is about risk and should be used for insuring against the risk of a catastrophic event. Such an insurance plan with a high deductible and in a competitive insurance environment could be moderate in price.

ENTITLEMENTS AND health care reform. Those are among the hardest domestic policy issues we face in this country, but they are arguably the most important ones too—they shouldn't be avoided. Another illustration from the construction business describes the nature of this challenge. Say that you ask me to build a bridge across the Potomac River: I can do the soil tests, order the steel, sink the foundations, and soon I have a bridge built that you can drive a truck over. Job done. But if you instead say to me, "Build the bridge such that there are no lost time accidents during construction," and my response is to put up some guard rails, thinking I've solved the problem, then I've lost. Because now it's not a *soluble* problem—it's the kind of problem you have to *work at.*

For progress here, and on public spending elsewhere, ramming through a new law or executive order is not success. Like many of the priorities in this *Blueprint*, the real governance challenge is in getting the balance of the American people on board with the overall need and general direction from the start. "Guardrails" won't cut it, either. Instead, you will probably have to go about things afresh, with an essentially nonpartisan, problem-solving attitude. And if you work at it—professionally, creatively, and relentlessly day-by-day—you just might get that bridge built without a lost-time accident.

CHAPTER 2

ENTITLEMENTS AND THE BUDGET

John F. Cogan

The United States faces a fiscal challenge unlike any in its history. The annual federal budget deficit routinely exceeds $400 billion. Without any legislative change, it is expected to remain at this level for the next few years. As large as these deficits may seem, their true magnitude is masked by abnormally low current interest payments on the national debt. If the average interest rate on the debt were at the level of its prior sixty-year average, the current and near-term annual budget deficit would be $800 billion.

The future fiscal challenge is far more severe. Federal spending increases are projected to cause federal deficits to soar past the $1-trillion-per-year mark in ten years. At that point, the outstanding public debt would exceed the nation's output of goods and services. In twenty years, the expenditure growth is projected to push the publicly held federal debt to 150 percent of GDP. At that point, half of all federal income tax collections would be needed just to pay interest on the debt, and half of those taxes would be sent overseas to pay foreign holders of US debt.

Federal entitlement programs are the primary cause of the current and future fiscal situation. Throughout the post–World

---

Comments by Michael Boskin, John Cochrane, and George Shultz are gratefully acknowledged.

War II years, Congresses and presidents have created new entitlements and repeatedly expanded existing ones without regard to their fiscal consequences.

During these years, federal spending has risen from 15 percent to 21 percent of GDP (see figure 1). Entitlement spending alone accounts for all of this increase. Spending on national security, the federal workforce, and the vast complex of non-defense programs has actually declined as a share of the nation's output of goods and services. The growth in federal entitlement spending is about to accelerate, fueled by the 72-million-member baby boom generation's retirement. Unless action is taken soon, entitlement expenditures plus interest payments will consume all federal government tax revenues a dozen years from now.

Federal entitlement programs are often justified by the natural human impulse to help the poor, the elderly, and the disabled meet their health care, housing, nutrition, and other needs. But the complex network of entitlement programs has expanded far beyond this basic objective. The excesses are evident in a few num-

Figure 1. **Federal expenditures, 1950–2046**

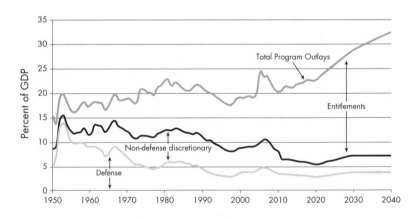

SOURCE Author's chart and calculations from Congressional Budget Office, The Long-Term Budget Outlook, December 2015, https://www.cbo.gov/publication/50250#title0.

bers. In 2013, the last year for which complete data are available, 56 percent of the US population lived in families that received assistance from at least one federal entitlement. Among the population living in families headed by persons under age sixty-five, the number is 46 percent. Similarly, the portion of the population receiving Social Security retirement benefits, Medicare, Medicaid, Social Security Disability Insurance, food stamps, Supplemental Security Income, and the earned income tax credit have all reached record highs. Entitlement benefits now flow mostly to middle-class Americans, paid for by middle-class Americans' taxes. Benefits provided to senior citizens have reached remarkably generous levels. The typical married couple that reaches Social Security's retirement age this year can expect to receive more than $1 million in Social Security and Medicare benefits, after adjusting for inflation, during their remaining lifetimes.

THE ESSENTIAL ELEMENTS OF ENTITLEMENT REFORM

The rapidly rising levels of federal spending and the national debt cannot be slowed without immediate legislative action to rein in entitlement spending. Major reductions in entitlement benefits or eligibility restrictions should come slowly and predictably. This is especially true for Social Security and Medicare changes to allow recipients sufficient time to make adjustments in planned retirement decisions. Policies to significantly alter either program's spending trajectory ten years from now must be put in place soon and be allowed to gradually take effect. History shows that a failure to act in advance of an entitlement-funding crisis inevitably results in higher taxes.

Three policies taken together would put Social Security on an affordable path. *First*, benefit increases paid to future cohorts of retirees should be limited to the rate of inflation. Under a mistaken "wage-indexing" policy put in place four decades ago, the inflation-adjusted value of Social Security benefits rises from one cohort of retirees to the next. This means the average worker who is age fifty today can expect to receive a monthly Social Security benefit that is about 15 percent higher than today's typical new retiree after adjusting for inflation. The average twenty-five-year-old worker today is promised an inflation-adjusted monthly benefit that is 36 percent higher. The United States can afford the current level of benefits, but not the promised increases. The proposed "price-indexing" policy would ensure that typical future retirees receive monthly Social Security benefits whose purchasing power is no less than that of today's typical retirees.

Second, Social Security's normal retirement age should be gradually increased and combined with a policy to encourage older workers to remain employed. The latter could be accomplished by eliminating payroll taxes on the earnings of workers once they have reached Social Security's retirement age. Eliminating the payroll tax would acknowledge that workers reaching Social Security's retirement age are "paid up" and, at the same time, it would provide a greater incentive for older workers who are capable of continued work to remain employed.

Third, younger workers should be allowed to invest a portion of their payroll taxes in safe, broadly diversified, stock and bond funds. Such a policy would create greater incentives for young persons to save and invest for retirement. It would allow younger workers to retire as millionaires through their own hard work and thrift, rather than from income taken from younger workers through taxation.

Slowing the growth in Medicare benefits is more difficult, but it can be achieved with a few simple policies. Moving away from Medicare's fee-for-service system and low copayments is essential. Under these policies, every time a senior citizen meets with his or her physician or other health care provider for a check-up, receives a lab test or undergoes surgery, or is admitted to a hospital, somebody other than the patient foots most of the bill. That such a program should produce runaway costs is hardly surprising. The federal government's main response to the program's soaring cost—price controls on physicians and hospitals—has only exacerbated the problem. Predictably, the price controls have already begun to make it harder for seniors to find doctors who are willing to treat them.

Medicare should be transformed gradually from its current form of an acute-care program into a true insurance program that offers greater financial protection against the high cost of catastrophic illness. Medicare recipients should be given vouchers to enable them to buy affordable private insurance plans from a menu of choices. Although this policy might seem radical, it is not. Currently, 25 percent of all Medicare recipients are enrolled in Medicare Advantage programs, which pay private health plans a fixed amount for each enrollee. A similar policy currently governs the entire Medicare prescription drug program. The voucher proposal would give patients the ability to choose among health plans—just as they now choose among Medicare prescription drug plans—and it would sweep away the need for any and all of Medicare's current 10,000 individual price controls. Competition among health care providers, not government-administered prices and government boards of experts making coverage decisions, is the best way to ensure high quality and reasonably priced health care.

Cost-consciousness among Medicare recipients could be greatly improved by modestly increasing Medicare premiums and copayments for routine services. Premiums paid by senior citizens once covered half of the cost of Medicare physician and related services. They now cover only one-fourth. Copayments that once covered nearly 40 percent of Medicare physician costs now cover less than 20 percent. The conversion of Medicare into a true insurance program should be completed by allowing Medicare health plans to cover catastrophic health care costs. Such a policy would afford Medicare recipients, a significant portion of whom have nontrivial financial assets, a more appropriate insurance protection. These reforms will not only save taxpayer money, they will ultimately give seniors greater access to cost-effective medical care than the existing program's combination of low copayments and increased rationing.

Responsibility for welfare programs should be transferred back to the states with significantly less federal funding. The federal welfare role began in the 1930s when the federal government first provided limited financial assistance to state-run welfare programs for persons who were unable to work. This limited role has metastasized into a massive $700-billion complex of federal programs that now delivers entitlement benefits to households with incomes far in excess of the poverty line. Coupled with this aid are severe financial penalties that discourage work and human capital investments by recipients.

The highly successful 1996 reform of the controversial Aid to Families with Dependent Children program, at the time the main welfare program for single mothers with children (now named Temporary Assistance for Needy Families), provides the model for transferring authority for welfare to the states. The reform law eliminated the entitlement to AFDC, established a federal block grant to financially assist states, and gave states virtually complete authority to set eligibility rules and benefit levels. Since the reform law's enactment, states have moved millions of welfare mothers from a dead-end life of dependency on government assistance to one of self-sufficiency through work. Since 1996, the number of families dependent on AFDC has declined by 60 percent, two-thirds of AFDC mothers have left the welfare program to obtain productive employment, and poverty rates among single-female-headed households with children have declined. This same approach should be applied to food stamps, child nutrition programs, Supplemental Security Income, housing subsidies, Medicaid, and other welfare programs.

As with Social Security and Medicare, discussions about welfare are too often ideological. Reformers are incorrectly cast as heartless people who are unwilling to help the less fortunate. State governments are erroneously cast as uncaring entities that seek to offload the cost of assistance on neighboring states. An effective welfare reform, like the AFDC reform, improves the actual outcomes for the targeted citizens. Welfare reform should be judged on such results. By this standard alone, returning the welfare system to the states is long overdue.

THE IMPORTANCE OF ECONOMIC GROWTH

Entitlement reform, though necessary, can reduce the growth in spending by only so much. Policies to increase economic growth must also be a central part of any plan for entitlements. How important is economic growth? Recent history provides a powerful demonstration. Between 1982 and 2001, federal spending, adjusted for inflation, increased by 50 percent. Yet over the same period, the amount of national income that was required to finance this spending declined from 23 cents to 18 cents per dollar. This occurred because inflation-adjusted national income, bolstered by a 3.4 percent average annual real growth rate, nearly doubled during the period. The economic policy recipe that helped produce this growth consisted of sharply lower personal and business income tax rates, disciplined restraint on federal spending, reduced federal regulation of labor and commerce, lower international trade barriers, and a stable, rules-based, monetary policy. A return to these policies must be part of any effort to address the federal government's entitlement problem.

CHAPTER 3

A BLUEPRINT FOR TAX REFORM

Michael J. Boskin

The primary purpose of taxation should be to raise the revenue necessary to finance government spending. Federal spending is projected to grow rapidly in coming decades. The primary drivers are the increased costs of entitlements such as Social Security and Medicare (due primarily to rising real outlays per beneficiary—demography plays an important but minority role) and higher interest costs on the growing debt.

In order to cover the cost of projected spending, say, in 2040, income and/or payroll tax rates would have to rise so much that many middle-income families would face marginal tax rates over 60 percent. That would make most American workers minority partners in their own (marginal) labor, a recipe for stagnation. So reforming the current tax system must be complemented by spending control; otherwise, even a more efficient reformed tax system will eventually be undone.

The borders between taxation, spending, and regulation are blurry. A regulatory requirement on a business or household usually imposes costs and requires some compliance. For example, a regulation requiring car companies to install airbags in cars drives up the cost of the car. It may well have benefits that exceed the costs, but the costs show up as part of private auto sales, thereby making the government appear smaller, even though the regulation is quite similar to the government collecting a tax and paying companies to install the airbags. The mandate requiring companies to provide health insurance for full-time employees, likewise, is like a tax used to pay for health insurance. Estimates of the annual cost of federal regulations substantially exceed $1 trillion per year.

As negative taxes in the form of refundable credits have proliferated and grown, the dividing line between taxes and spending can be elusive. The convention used in the federal budget is that the part of the credit that reduces a positive tax liability is a reduction in taxes, whereas any negative net refund component is considered an outlay.

We all know that the tax code is riddled with special features—deductions, credits, and the like—which greatly reduce revenue while promoting, or at least appearing to promote, various activities, some quite popular. These so-called tax expenditures—such as the mortgage interest deduction or the electric car credit —severely erode the tax base and reduce tax revenue by over $1 trillion per year. So it is useful to keep spending and regulation in mind in any discussion of taxation.

Finally, while governments may also borrow, the debt must be repaid or refinanced, and in either case will require higher future taxes for any given level of spending.

Taxes distort many important economic decisions. For example, taxes lower economic growth, because our tax system reduces incentives to save and invest; to work and acquire skills; and to engage in entrepreneurship. Taxes also distort the allocation of capital and labor among uses of differing productivity. While other policies—regulatory, trade, educational, training, immigration, and monetary—affect growth, our tax and spending, and therefore debt, policies are likely to be the most important.

By reducing after-tax wages and returns to saving, the income tax decreases work and saving. The corporate income tax discourages capital formation, encourages excessive leverage by companies and banks, and reallocates capital by industry and sector with its numerous special provisions. These biases assure that overall capital formation runs steeply uphill, while some investments run more, some less uphill. It would be comical if the deleterious consequences weren't so severe. Every introductory economics student learns that the harm from these distortions rises with the square of the tax rate (this derives from the area under supply and demand curves). Doubling the rate quadruples the harm. Thus, the primary goal of taxation should be to raise the revenue to finance the necessary functions of government in the least distortionary manner possible.

These economic distortions depend on the combined overall rate of taxation for each activity. The same activity may be taxed multiple times. For example, wages may be taxed under the federal personal income tax, the Social Security payroll tax, the Medicare payroll tax, and state income taxes; when the wages are spent, sales taxes might be levied. Saving is generally taxed twice under the income tax, first when the income out of which the saving occurs is earned and saved, and then again when it earns a return in the form of interest or dividends. The corporate tax is an additional tax on capital income. For those with sizable estates, the estate tax adds yet another tax on saving.

Most states add another layer of personal and corporate income taxation. While this discussion of tax reform focuses on the federal personal and corporate income taxes, as do most reform proposals, it is necessary to keep these other taxes in mind. For example, for the most productive California citizens and successful small businesses (which are taxed at personal rates), marginal tax rates exceed 50 percent, not just the 39.6 percent federal rate.

As a result of these distortions, a dollar of additional revenue costs the economy about $1.40. Reducing the harm from these tax distortions is the main reason to keep marginal tax rates as low as possible while raising sufficient revenue to fund the necessary functions of government. Thus, tax systems with low rates and broad bases are the most effective foundation for an efficient, growing economy.

The United States has the highest corporate tax rate of any

advanced economy—39 percent including state taxes, or 50 percent higher than the OECD (Organisation for Economic Cooperation and Development) average. Of course, various credits and deductions—such as for depreciation and interest—reduce the effective corporate tax rate, but it is still out of line with our global competitors. Corporate income is taxed a second time at the personal level as dividends, or capital gains if the company retains and reinvests the earnings. It is important that the corporate rate and the top personal rate be quite similar, if not identical. When even a modest gap arises, huge volumes of capital will shift in or out of the corporate organizational form, depending on which rate is lowest, in order to legally avoid the higher tax.

Corporations do not pay taxes; people do. The corporations remit them, but in the final analysis, it is people who pay them, as consumers in higher prices, workers in lower wages, or investors in lower returns. In a static economy with no international trade, the corporate tax would likely be borne by shareholders or owners of capital more generally. The US economy is neither static nor closed, and taxes tend to be borne by the least mobile (elastic) factor of production. Capital is much more globally mobile than labor, and the part of the corporate tax that is above that of our lowest-tax major competitors will eventually be borne by American workers. That burden is larger in a growing economy, as the lower investment slows productivity growth and future wage increases.

There is considerable evidence that high corporate taxes are economically dangerous. The OECD concludes that "corporate taxes are found to be most harmful for growth, followed by personal income tax, and then consumption taxes." Many of the problems of our tax system result from the attempt to tax income, including investment returns, rather than consumption. Income taxes are inevitably far more complex and easier to avoid or evade.

So it is not surprising that virtually every major tax reform proposal in recent decades has centered on lowering tax rates and moving toward a broad-based, low-rates tax primarily on consumption. Consumption can be taxed directly, as in a sales or value-added tax, or by deducting saving and investment from income in determining the tax base, a consumed income tax. There are numerous ways this can be accomplished, for example, by junking the separate corporate income tax, integrating it with the personal income tax by attributing corporate income and taxes to shareholders, or eliminating personal taxes on corporate distributions, and allowing an immediate tax deduction, so-called expensing, for investment (net of interest), which cancels the tax at the margin on new investment.

Four decades of Treasury proposals, the 2005 President's Tax Commission Proposals, and the Simpson-Bowles Commission, appointed and subsequently ignored by President Obama, all moved in that direction. Proposals such as the Hall-Rabushka flat tax; Bradford's progressive consumption tax, a version of which was introduced some years ago by senators Sam Nunn and Pete Domenici; a value-added tax (VAT); and the "FairTax" retail sales tax are pure consumption taxes. There is considerable research showing that moving toward a broad-based, integrated progressive consumption tax would significantly increase real GDP and future wages. Replacing both the corporate and personal income taxes with a broad, revenue-neutral consumption or consumed income tax would produce even larger gains. In his presidential address to the American Economic Association, Nobel Laureate Robert Lucas concluded that implementing such reforms would deliver great benefits, raising income 7 percent to 15 percent, at little cost, making it "the largest genuinely true free lunch I have seen."

The main danger of a broad-based consumption tax is that it will be added on top of other taxes, with the additional revenue used to grow government substantially. That risks serious erosion of our long-run standard of living. The VAT, for example, has been used for that purpose in Europe; and, while better than still-higher income taxes, the larger-size governments it has enabled are the prime reason European living standards are 30 percent or more lower than ours. Trading a good tax reform for a much larger government is beyond foolish. No tax reform can offset losses that large. Hence, new tax devices should only be on the table if they are not only revenue-neutral to start, but also accompanied by rigorous, enforceable spending controls.

The current personal and corporate income taxes have bases which are hybrids of income and consumption, given partial "consumption tax" features such as accelerated depreciation deductions and tax-deferred saving in individual retirement accounts and 401(k) accounts. But various limits, exclusions, and other features leave high rates on some types of saving and investment, low rates on others. I personally prefer a progressive, broad-based consumed income tax, but that raises the question of how to broaden the base. As noted above, tax expenditures cost the Treasury over $1 trillion per year. Removing or capping most would allow economically beneficial lower marginal tax rates. The difficulty of removing deductions and credits one by one is that each is backed by a powerful entrenched vested interest, and many are widely popular. As former Senate Finance Chair Russell Long famously put it, to most people tax reform means, "Don't tax you, don't tax me, tax the fellow behind the tree."

The 1986 Tax Reform Act demonstrated that sweeping reform with lower rates and a broader base is possible. Other important criteria for a good tax system include limiting its administrative and compliance costs and need for a phalanx of tax lawyers, accountants, and lobbyists that accompany complex tax rules. The President's Advisory Panel on Federal Tax Reform estimated in 2005 that the administrative and compliance costs exceeded $140 billion per year, and it is undoubtedly considerably larger now. A broader-based, lower-rate consumed income tax would considerably reduce this burden. A pure flat tax, a pure retail sales tax, and a pure VAT would do even better, but only if enacted as a replacement for current taxes. If added on, these costs would increase.

In addition to raising revenues to pay for government spending, the tax system also redistributes income. The current income tax system is very progressive. The top 1 percent of taxpayers, with 20 percent of income, pays 38 percent of all federal income taxes collected; the bottom 50 percent pays 2 to 3 percent of total income tax collections. Indeed, the OECD declares the US tax system the most progressive of any OECD nation. That is because most other nations rely on the slightly regressive value-added tax for a large share of their larger revenue as a share of GDP. Consumption-type tax reforms can be designed to maintain considerable progressivity, most easily in the consumed income tax, which can be levied at more than one rate, while providing a personal exemption. For example, an archetypical plan might have a few rates ranging from 5 percent to 25 percent on (consumed) income above the poverty rate, combined with a corporate rate of 25 percent.

In addition to the effects on efficiency, equity, and growth, it is also worth asking political economy questions. Will tax reform affect the size of government or its nature? As noted above, the value-added tax has been a prime enabler of larger government. Will the reform affect federalism? Some reforms risk encroaching on state and local revenue sources, of which the retail sales tax is often the largest.

Will the reform likely endure? We have had more than a dozen major, and many more minor, tax law changes since the landmark 1986 tax reform, many eroding the base or raising the rates. We should be concerned that we might move to a better tax system only to undo it shortly thereafter. Simplicity, transparency, and a common rate or rates are more promising than high rates, which breed tax avoidance or even outright evasion and undermine public confidence. The tax system not only changes often, but is riddled with dozens of temporary features which need to be debated and renewed every year. Congresses (and presidents) seem unable to avoid continually tinkering with the tax code. A tax reform that is filled with special features would lose much of its economic benefit. We need a stable tax system that changes much less frequently, so families and firms can more reliably plan for the future.

Finally, will the reform contribute to a prosperous, stable democracy? Will it help increase American wages and the living standards of the majority of the population? We need a larger fraction of economic activity paying taxes on a broader base that would enable lower rates. And we need a larger fraction of people participating in and benefiting from the economy and the financing of the necessary functions of government. Toward that end, a modest minimum income tax, payable by all, might be desirable. Reforming the personal and corporate income taxes into an integrated, progressive consumed income tax could contribute substantially to achieving these goals. A dramatic simplification of the tax code along these lines would also help reassure citizens that the system is not engineered so that special interests and the well-connected can avoid taxes. A tax system reliant on voluntary compliance must be, and must appear to be, fair and reasonable, not a vehicle for crony capitalism, to support a healthy democracy.

CHAPTER 4

TRANSFORMATIONAL
HEALTH CARE REFORM

Scott W. Atlas

The Affordable Care Act (ACA), frequently referred to as Obamacare, has pushed health care in the United States onto a drastically different, far more government-dominated pathway. In place now are a costly expansion of already failing entitlement programs, harmful new tax burdens, and unprecedented regulatory authority of the federal government over health insurance and the health care industry. These changes were instituted while ignoring, even doubling down on, the fundamental problems with the existing system—the perverse incentives that have caused runaway costs and excluded millions of Americans from the world's best medical care.

Years after the initial rollout of the ACA, the American people, the health care industry, and the courts still struggle to navigate the law. Time is of the essence. Under the new regulatory environment, consolidation has accelerated within virtually all of the important sectors of health care, including hospitals and physician practices, pharmaceutical companies, and insurers. This reduces competition, hurts consumers, and raises prices to patients by thousands of dollars per year.[1] Further implementation of the ACA will undoubtedly accelerate the development of a two-tiered health care system seen in other nationalized systems, and reverse the superior access and outstanding quality of care that distinguish American health care from the centralized systems that are failing the world over.

Meanwhile, Americans will increasingly require medical care at an unprecedented level, as the population ages and risk factors like obesity continue to compound. To meet these demands, technological advances in clinically relevant molecular biology, medical devices, and targeted pharmaceuticals offer great promise for new treatments and breakthrough cures. Yet the current trajectory of the health system, particularly under the ACA, threatens both the sustainability of the system and the essential climate for the innovation necessary to reach its potential.

I propose a comprehensive, six-point plan for reforming US health care (for a more detailed discussion, see Scott W. Atlas, *Restoring Quality Health Care: A Six-Point Plan for Comprehensive Reform at Lower Cost*, Hoover Institution Press, 2016): it would fundamentally transform the system by empowering consumers and instilling appropriate incentives to induce market-based competition, while reducing the federal government's authority over health care. My plan centers on instilling incentives for lower-cost insurance coverage and broadly expanded, universal health savings accounts. The plan restores the original purpose of health insurance: to protect against the risk of significant and unexpected health care costs. With these reforms, the plan enhances the availability and affordability of twenty-first-century medical care for all Americans, ensures continued innovation, and reduces health care costs by trillions of dollars over the decade. These savings will promote increased economic activity into other areas of the economy. Perhaps most importantly, the reforms in this plan reflect the key principles held by the American people about what they value and expect from health care in terms of access, choice, and quality.

This essay will examine the status of American health care in light of the ACA and then outline key reforms needed to meet the significant health care challenges facing the nation. Six major reforms are proposed, each with its underlying rationale: 1) expand affordable private insurance; 2) establish and liberalize universal health savings accounts to leverage consumer power; 3) introduce appropriate incentives with rational tax treatment of health spending; 4) modernize Medicare for the twenty-first century as the population ages; 5) overhaul Medicaid and eliminate the two-tiered system for poor Americans; and 6) strategically enhance the supply of medical care while ensuring innovation.

HEALTH CARE TODAY: SETTING THE RECORD STRAIGHT

America is facing its greatest health care challenges in history. Unprecedented demand for medical care is a certainty. The number of Americans sixty-five and older has increased by a full six million in the past decade alone to over 13 percent of the overall population, while those eighty-five and older have increased by a factor of ten from the 1950s to today's six million. Older people harbor the most disabling diseases, including heart disease, cancer, stroke, and dementia—the diseases that depend most on specialists and complex technology for diagnosis and treatment. Simultaneously, obesity, America's most serious health problem, has increased to crisis levels, already affecting more adults and children in the United States than in any other nation. Given the known lag time for such risk factors to affect health, the next decades promise to reveal obesity's massive cumulative health and economic harms.

These daunting demographic realities combine with serious fiscal challenges that promise to worsen in the absence of change. America's national health expenditures now total over $3.1 trillion per year, or more than 17.4 percent of GDP, and are projected to reach 19.6 percent of GDP by 2024.[2] Medicaid has expanded to cover over 70 million people[3] at a cost of $500 billion per year. Medicare spends over $260 billion annually on hospital benefits alone and $615 billion in total for 52 million enrollees. Workers paying taxes for the program will decline to 2.3 per beneficiary by 2030,[4] half of the number at Medicare's inception. With the aging of the baby boom generation, the program is unsustainable. Medicare's hospitalization insurance trust fund will face depletion in 2030. Barring changes, by 2049, federal expenditures for health care and Social Security are projected to consume all federal revenues, eliminating capacity for national defense, interest on the debt, or any other domestic program.[5]

At the same time, we have entered an extraordinary era in medical diagnosis and therapy. Innovative applications of molecular biology, advanced medical technologies, and new drug discoveries promise earlier diagnoses and safer, more effective cures. The possibilities of improving health through medical advances have never been greater.

Before designing reforms to achieve the promise of twenty-first-century health care for Americans, it is essential to understand the state of US health care before the ACA. Americans enjoyed unrivalled access to care,[6] whether defined by preventive screening tests; waiting times for diagnosis and specialists; treatment for chronic diseases; timeliness of biopsies for cancer and life-changing surgeries; or availability of safer technology and the newest drugs that save lives. The leading medical journals prove that American medical care delivers exceptional results for virtually all of the most serious diseases. That includes survival for cancer, outcomes from heart disease and stroke treatment, and treatment of chronic diseases such as hypertension and diabetes—all better than in those countries with government-centralized health systems.[7] The inescapable conclusion based on the facts is that both quality of medical care and the access to it have been superior in the United States than in those nationalized systems heralded as models for change by ACA supporters.

Partly based on now discredited studies[8] alleging the poor quality of America's health care, the ACA was enacted. Its two core elements, a significant Medicaid expansion and subsidies for exchange-based private insurance, will each cost close to one trillion dollars over the next decade.[9] Fundamentally, the ACA consists of a huge centralization of health care and health insurance to the federal government, driving government control of health insurance to unprecedented levels while dramatically pushing up private insurance premiums. During the first three quarters of 2014, 89 percent of the newly insured under the ACA were enrollees into Medicaid, not private insurance.[10] Coupled with population aging, Centers for Medicare and Medicaid Services projects that the 107 million under Medicaid or Medicare in 2013 will rapidly increase to 135 million just five years later, a growth rate tripling that of private insurance.[11]

But the goals of health reform demand quite the opposite. Facts show that private insurance is superior to government insurance for both access and quality of medical care (see next section). History shows that the best way to control prices is through competition for empowered, value-seeking consumers. Instead of shunting more people into insurance and care provided by, heavily subsidized by, or massively regulated by the government, reforms should focus on how to deliver innovation and cost savings, thereby maximizing the availability and affordability of the best care for everyone. The key is to move away from hyper-regulated centralized models relying on misguided incentives necessitating more and more taxation to competition-driven markets that will respond to empowered consumers incentivized to seek value.

REFORMING HEALTH CARE TO INCREASE ACCESS, AFFORDABILITY, AND EXCELLENCE

Reform 1: Expand Affordable Private Insurance

The Importance of Private Health Insurance
Broad access to doctors and hospitals comes through private, not government, insurance. The harsh reality awaiting low-income Americans is that doctors already refuse new Medicaid patients in numbers that dwarf by eight to ten *times* the percentage that refuses new private insurance patients.[12] As of 2014, 55 percent of

doctors in major metropolitan areas refused new Medicaid patients.[13] Even of those managed care providers signed by contract and on state lists to provide care to Medicaid enrollees, 51 percent are not available to new Medicaid patients.[14] Likewise, about one-quarter of doctors no longer see Medicare patients or limit the number they see; in primary care, 34 percent refuse Medicare.[15] The percentage of doctors who closed their practices to Medicare or Medicaid by 2012 had increased by 47 percent since 2008.[16]

The quality of medical outcomes is also superior with private insurance. For those with private insurance, that includes fewer in-hospital deaths, fewer complications from surgery, longer survival after treatment, and shorter hospital stays than similar patients with government insurance.[17] It is highly likely that restricted access to important drugs, specialists, and technology under government insurance accounts for these differences.

The Harmful Impact of the ACA on Private Insurance

As a direct result of the ACA's new mandates and pricing regulations, the law has already forced more than five million Americans off their existing private plans. The Congressional Budget Office (CBO) projects that a stunning ten million Americans will be forced off their chosen employer-based health insurance by 2021—a *ten-fold increase* in the number that was initially projected back in 2011.[18] Meanwhile, private insurance premiums have greatly increased under the ACA and are projected to sky-rocket in 2016, in some cases increasing by 30 percent to 50 percent and more. Additionally, because government reimbursement for care is often below cost, costs are shifted back to private carriers, further escalating private premiums. Nationally, the gap between private insurance payment and government underpayment has become the widest in twenty years, doubling since the ACA began.[19] More ominously, consolidation among the five big private insurers is accelerating; most believe this will further raise premiums for individuals and small businesses. This not only impacts the individual, but all taxpayers, because all taxpayers subsidize those higher premiums via ACA insurance subsidies.

Private insurance choices and providers covered under them are dwindling as well. As of December 2014,[20] the exchanges offered 21 percent fewer plans than the pre-ACA individual market nationally. For those dependent on subsidized insurance through government exchanges, narrower provider networks doubled in 2013 since the previous year (although perhaps stabilizing in 2014).[21] Exchange plans in 2015 restricted access to doctors and hospitals far more than plans bought off exchanges,[22] and they completely exclude many top cancer hospitals and important specialists[23] in an attempt to quell premium increases caused by the law itself.

Keys to Expanding Affordable Private Insurance

The ACA has made private insurance less affordable and pushed health insurance reform in the wrong direction. It has furthered the erroneous view that insurance should subsidize the entire gamut of medical services, including routine medical care. American consumers, though, have demonstrated that higher deductible coverage generates more affordable insurance and reduces health spending.[24] Consumer spending has decreased with high deductible plans,[25] without any consequent increases in emergency room visits or hospitalizations and without harmful impact on economically vulnerable families.[26] In studies, more than one-third of the savings reflected lower costs per health care utilization,[27] i.e., value-based decision-making by consumers. Additional evidence from magnetic resonance imaging (MRI)[28] and outpatient surgery[29] shows that introducing price transparency and defined-contribution benefits further encourages price comparisons by patients. The evidence shows that given the opportunity, consumers make value-based decisions when purchasing health care.

Fundamental change to private insurance is vital to leveraging consumer power and expanding affordable health care. It is first essential to reduce onerous regulations on insurance. While consumers are still increasingly opting for plans with deductibles greater than $2,000, the growth rates have slowed compared to before ACA mandates and regulations.[30] We should eliminate unnecessary coverage mandates that have ballooned under the ACA, including so-called "minimum essential benefits" that have increased premiums by almost 10 percent[31] as well as many of the more than 2,270 state mandates[32] requiring coverage for everything from acupuncture to marriage therapy. We should also remove obstacles to competition, including archaic barriers to out-of-state insurance purchases, and restore pre-ACA actuarial restrictions on age-rated premiums to eliminate unfair cost shifts imposed by the ACA that raised premiums for younger, healthier enrollees by 19 percent to 35 percent.[33] Finally, we should repeal the ACA's added health insurance providers fee that insurers pass on to enrollees through increased premiums ($11.3 billion in 2015).[34]

Health insurance reform is also a powerful opportunity to encourage healthy lifestyles, especially since three-fourths of health insurance claims may be due to lifestyle choices.[35] Cigarette smoking causes $193 billion in direct health care expenditures and productivity losses each year, according to the Centers for Disease Control.[36] Annual medical costs for people who are obese were $1,429 higher in 2006 than for those of normal weight; for Medicare patients, this difference was $1,723, with almost 40 percent due to extra prescription drugs.[37] Extra medical care for obesity alone comprises up to 10 percent of total US health care costs,[38] while its total US societal costs exceed $215 billion per year.[39] While smoking has declined, the burden of obesity to the health care system and to all taxpayers continues to increase. Just as in other insurance, premiums that reflect higher risks from voluntary behavior, such as obesity and smoking, are sensible.

Reform 2: Establish and Liberalize
Universal Health Savings Accounts

Health savings accounts (HSAs) allow individuals to set aside money tax-free for uncovered expenses, including routine care. Despite the ACA's restrictions, HSAs continue to grow, with a one-year jump of 29 percent as of the end of 2014, reaching a record 14.5 million in mid-2015.[40] Nearly one-third of all employers (31 percent) now offer some type of HSA, up from just 4 percent since 2005. By the end of 2017, the HSA market will surpass $46 billion in assets held in almost 25 million accounts.

Expanding HSAs with high deductible coverage reduces health care costs. System-wide health expenditures would fall by an estimated $57 billion per year if even half of Americans with employer-sponsored insurance enrolled in plans combining HSAs with high deductibles.[41] Savings would increase further if deductibles were truly high, e.g., $4,000 to $5,000, and if these plans were freed from the added costly mandates of the ACA.

The issue is not whether these accounts are effective; it is how to maximize their adoption and eliminate the government rules that serve as obstacles to their use. First, HSAs should be available to all Americans, regardless of age and without any requirement of specific insurance deductible. We should significantly increase ACA-defined HSA maximums, ease restrictions on their uses, and allow rollovers to surviving family members. We should also remove ACA-specified limits to financial incentives from employers, including deposits into employee HSAs, to increase these powerful motivators for employees to participate in wellness programs already proven to benefit workers and firms by improving health and reducing health costs.[42]

Reform 3: Introduce Appropriate Incentives
with Rational Tax Treatment of Health Spending

The income tax subsidy for unlimited health spending creates harmful incentives for consumers that are counterproductive to competition and pricing, replaces higher take-home wages, and is highly regressive,[43] preferentially giving high-income earners more tax breaks. The largest tax subsidy—the exclusion from income and payroll taxes of employer and employee contributions for employer-sponsored insurance—costs approximately $250 billion in lost federal tax revenue in 2013.[44] In addition, the federal tax deduction for health expenses (including premiums) exceeding 10 percent of the adjusted gross income is estimated to have cost $12.4 billion in lost tax revenue in 2014.[45]

Beyond the numbers, the tax exclusion creates perverse incentives counterproductive to consumer empowerment and competitive pricing. The exclusion makes health spending seem less expensive than it is, encouraging more expensive insurance policies with more elaborate coverage as well as higher demand for medical care, regardless of cost. The distortion of health insurance to cover almost all billable services, while minimizing direct payment by patients, is partly attributable to the tax preference. This has greatly increased the overall cost of health care.[46]

Under the ACA, the tax exclusion will change in 2018. A new excise tax will be imposed on employment-based health benefits whose total value is greater than specified thresholds. (The Joint Committee on Taxation and the CBO project that 2018 thresholds will be $10,200 for single coverage and $27,500 for family coverage.) The excise tax will be equal to 40 percent of the difference between the total value of tax-excluded contributions and the threshold. But allowing a government to impose new, high taxes on products whose prices became unnecessarily high directly because of the government's policies is not only bad for consumers but frankly absurd.

Changing the tax treatment of health spending is an important part of urgently needed health care reforms; unfortunately, comprehensive tax reform into a broad-based, low-rate, simple system seems unlikely at this time. Given that reality, tax reforms should eliminate the ACA excise tax and incorporate a number of important features, including: 1) universality, regardless of the source of health benefits and independent of employment; 2) limits on total allowed exclusion; and 3) new criteria on eligible spending for tax exclusion, such as only catastrophic coverage and HSA funding. Such tax reforms would realign incentives to encourage value-based health care purchasing and ultimately lower the cost of health care.

Reform 4: Modernize Medicare for the Twenty-first Century

Medicare is an antiquated, labyrinthine system designed for decades long past, and it is in serious financial trouble. The population of seniors is dramatically expanding, while the taxpayer base financing the program is dramatically shrinking. Nearly four million Americans now reach age sixty-five every year; in 2050, this population will reach 83.7 million. Americans live 25 percent longer after age sixty-five now than in 1972,[47] about five years longer than at the inception of Medicare. Today's seniors need to save money for decades, not just years, of future health care.

Despite the expanding needs, the ACA imposed a new obstacle to health care for seniors. Its Independent Payment Advisory Board, a group of political appointees, is specifically tasked with formulaically reducing payments to doctors and hospitals. And contrary to the administration's demonization of private insurers, Medicare already ranks at the top of the charts for the highest rates of claim refusals—more than nearly all comparable private insurers every year.[48] Meanwhile, doctors are increasingly refusing traditional Medicare, and this promises to accelerate.[49] Without significant change, seniors will have serious difficulty finding medical care; soon, Medicare will mirror the two-tiered system seen routinely in other nationalized systems, where only the affluent can circumvent the system.

Seniors have shown the path toward Medicare reform—more than 70 percent of beneficiaries already supplement or replace traditional Medicare with private insurance. Voluntary enrollment in alternative Medicare Advantage, private health plans competing for business, has expanded to 31 percent of beneficiaries, tripling since 2004 to 16.8 million in 2015. Private prescription drug coverage in Part D has also been highly favored by beneficiaries.

To fix Medicare and prevent the collapse of this crucial safety net, we need to empower seniors—the heaviest users of health care—to seek and receive value. Modernizing Medicare for the twenty-first century centers on a three-pronged strategy: 1) increasing private insurance options for beneficiaries with competition-based premiums and integrated benefits, as well as consumer incentives to seek value; 2) expanding the eligibility and uses of large HSAs that share all features and limits with HSAs outside of Medicare; and 3) updating eligibility from the obsolete criteria of fifty years ago to reflect the demographics and health needs of today's seniors.

Reform 5: Overhaul Medicaid and Eliminate the Two-tiered System for Poor Americans

Instead of providing a pathway to excellent health care for poor Americans, the ACA's expansion of Medicaid continues and even exacerbates their second-class health care status, at a cost of $500 billion per year to taxpayers that rises to $890 billion in 2024.[50] As an alternative, a few states have taken the lead via special waivers to facilitate a transition into private coverage with better access to medical care. Arkansas and Iowa have received approval to use the "private option" in which Medicaid provides premium assistance to purchase private plans in lieu of direct Medicaid coverage.[51] Additionally, Michigan and Indiana have added HSA options for Medicaid beneficiaries, and Arkansas has begun the approval process. Although still burdened with a mandated set of benefits and other regulations under the ACA, these are steps in the right direction.

We should transform Medicaid into a bridge program geared toward enrolling beneficiaries into affordable private insurance

instead of funneling low-income families into substandard traditional Medicaid coverage. We should also establish and seed-fund
Medicaid HSAs that empower enrollees with the same control as
all other Americans, including incentives for good health. Federal
Medicaid funding via fixed dollar amounts to states should include incentives for states to ensure availability of private, lower-
cost catastrophic coverage to all Medicaid-eligible families as well
as to the entire state population; that funding should be contin-
gent on meeting certain enrollment thresholds for Medicaid beneficiaries into private coverage and HSAs. These incentive-based
Medicaid reforms could move Medicaid enrollees to private coverage, with access to the same doctors, specialists, treatments, and
medical technology as the general population, thereby eliminating the two-tiered health system that the ACA furthers.

**Reform 6: Strategically Enhance the Supply
of Medical Care While Ensuring Innovation**
The challenges to health care access and cost cannot be met without strategically modernizing the supply and delivery of medical
care. Private-sector clinics staffed by nurse practitioners and physician assistants can provide routine primary care, including flu
shots, blood pressure monitoring, and blood tests. Care at retail
clinics is 30 percent to 40 percent cheaper than similar care at
physicians' offices and about 80 percent cheaper than at emergency departments,[52] potentially saving hundreds of millions of
dollars per year while increasing the availability of primary care.[53]
The key to encouraging the proliferation of these clinics rests on
preventing obstacles to their use, such as unnecessarily burden-
some documentation or overly complex insurance credentialing
requirements. Additionally, states should follow the recommendations of the Institute of Medicine[54] and remove outmoded
scope-of-practice limits and unfounded restrictions on nurse
practitioners and physician assistants.

States should also modernize physician licensing. Nonreciprocal licensing by states unnecessarily limits patient care, especially in our era of telemedicine. It is also time to relax tight limits that have stagnated medical school graduation numbers for almost forty years. Medical societies further harm consumers by artificially limiting the residency training positions and consequently restraining competition among doctors. These anti-consumer practices need to be open to public scrutiny and abolished. To alleviate the impending shortage of specialist doctors[55] who are trained to use advanced technology and further clinical innovation, we should rein in malpractice lawsuits with caps on noneconomic damages and encourage streamlined training programs when possible.

Perhaps the most insidious consequence of the ACA is the threat to innovation. The overwhelming majority of the world's health care innovation occurs in the United States, but that is changing. Growth of total US research and development (R&D) from 2012 to 2014 averaged only 2.1 percent, down from 6 percent over the previous fifteen years.[56] This has been exacerbated by more than $500 billion in new taxes over the ACA's first decade on device and drug manufacturers. Concurrently, Food and Drug Administration delays for approvals of new devices are now far longer than in Europe.[57]

What can be done to reverse these damaging trends? First, strip back the heavy tax burdens that inhibit innovation, starting with a permanent repeal of the ACA's $24 billion medical device excise tax and the $30 billion tax on brand-name drugs. Repeal the law's investment tax to restore tax incentives for funding early-stage technology and life science companies. Simplify processes for new device and drug approvals, including low-cost generics, so that the FDA becomes a favorable rather than an obstructionist environment. Finally, despite legitimate security concerns, targeted immigration reforms are needed to encourage educated, high-skill entrepreneurs to stay in America. A decade ago, from two-thirds to over 90 percent of foreign students in the United

States remained here, but today only 6 percent of Indian, 10 percent of Chinese, and 15 percent of European students expect to make America their permanent home.[58] Although partly due to improving opportunities in those students' home countries, lawmakers should take a fresh look at easing counterproductive immigration restrictions. New skill-based visa programs should be instituted that target highly educated individuals, particularly students completing American university graduate-degree programs in science and technology.

CONCLUSION

Paradoxically, as our nation is doubling down on government authority over health care, those countries with the longest experience of nationalized health care, from Britain to Denmark to Sweden, are shifting patients toward private health care to remedy their failed systems.[59] Likewise, Europeans with means or power are increasingly circumventing their centralized systems. Private insurance in the European Union has grown by more than 50 percent in the past decade.[60] In reaction to unconscionable waits for care,[61] about 11 percent of Britons, including almost two-thirds who earn more than $78,700, hold private insurance—even though they are already paying $175 billion in taxes for their "free" National Health Insurance[62] and despite the government's insurance premium tax to thwart its rise.[63] In Sweden, an average family pays nearly $20,000 annually in taxes toward health care, yet almost 600,000 Swedes also buy private insurance, a number that has increased by 67 percent over the last five years.[64] Unless the ACA is drastically altered, America's health care will mirror those systems and become even more divided with even more inequality, where ultimately only the lower and middle classes will suffer its full harm.

The debate in the United States should focus on what specific reforms are appropriate to fix the inadequacies and reduce the cost of American health care without jeopardizing its excellence.

Reforming US health care should specifically promote lower cost private insurance coverage and large, liberalized HSAs in order to expand market competition for better value and more consumer choices.

Voters overwhelmingly support such reforms. In answer to the question, "What would do more to reduce health care costs—more free market competition between insurance companies or more government regulation?" 62 percent of voters chose more free market competition, while only 26 percent chose more regulation.[65] A vast majority—a full 70 percent—say they have a right to choose between health plans that cost more and cover just about all medical procedures and other plans that cost less while covering only major procedures (only 18 percent are opposed).[66] An even greater majority, 80 percent to only 9 percent, say individuals should have the right to choose between plans that have higher deductibles and lower premiums versus plans with lower deductibles and higher premiums. It is the responsibility of government leaders to facilitate a health care system that reflects these important principles cherished by the American people.

CHAPTER 5

REFORMING REGULATION

Michael J. Boskin

Government regulation, at the federal, state, and local levels, is pervasive. Last year alone, almost eighty thousand pages of rules, proposed rules, and notices were published in the federal register. Most regulations impose costs, and studies indicate they cause a cumulative large drag on the economy. Those costs are colloquially said to be "on business," but in reality businesses shift them to consumers with higher prices, workers with lower wages, or investors with lower returns.

Regulations can also stifle innovation and competition, and therefore economic growth. In fact, most economic regulation keeps prices up and competition down, e.g., taxi regulation. Regulation can also achieve important social benefits, such as reducing pollution. Most of our laws, and Supreme Court rulings on federal agencies' implementation of laws, wisely demand a sensible balancing of these benefits with costs and risks. While estimates of regulatory costs and benefits are less precise than those for direct spending and taxation, studies from think tanks and government agencies estimate the annual cost of regulation at well over a trillion dollars per year. In 2014, the Office of Management and Budget reported that the cost of just the small fraction of new rules enacted in the prior decade, with estimated annual costs over $100 million, was $100 billion a year. But that includes only a handful of the more than thirty thousand regulations the

Office of Management and Budget (OMB) enumerates, and none of the costly, long-standing major regulations. And these cost estimates include only the direct costs of complying with regulation, not the potential lost innovation (e.g., new drugs that regulation inhibits) or the effects of reduced competition and delay. Some businesses operate in a straitjacket of rules and regulation; for example, a single refinery may confront twenty thousand different potential regulatory violations per day.

To be sure, there may be enough economic, health, safety, environmental, or other benefits to justify many regulations, and some sectors of the economy need regulation for various reasons. For most of the previous century, economic regulation of traditional natural monopolies—utilities in telecommunications, electricity, and transportation, for example—dominated the regulatory terrain. With large network fixed costs, demand—especially local demand—was insufficient to support more than one or a very few firms. To try to gain some of the benefits of competition, and to decrease monopoly or oligopoly pricing, these firms were regulated by utility commissions that set negotiated prices deemed sufficient to secure a reasonable return for the firm. Insufficient incentive was left to innovate, as firms had little upside. A couple of decades ago, productivity pricing requiring the firm to lower price(s) (net of inflation) by a modest productivity target created greater incentives to lower cost, especially since the firm, at least for some time, had upside return opportunities if it could beat the productivity target.

However, as Nobel Laureate George Stigler suggested, the regulators are often captured by the very industry they are regulating. The regulators depend on the regulated firms for information about costs and other factors. These firms have strong incentives to fashion information that benefits them and, perhaps more importantly, to encourage rules that protect them from competition, especially competition from new and innovative firms. Complex and time-consuming regulation itself limits competition. Dealing with regulation is a large fixed cost that has to be spread over a large base of customers, which a new entrant does not have. So obtaining all the necessary regulatory approvals can keep newcomers out.

Captured regulators may fail disastrously. A blatant example was that of the banking regulators, including the New York Federal Reserve, who at best were asleep at the wheel leading up to the financial crisis of 2008–09. In the middle of the last decade, in an attempt to ward off European Union regulation of American investment banks' European operations, the Securities and Exchange Commission took on regulating the investment banks. How did it do? It allowed them to increase their already-high leverage and measure their own capital!

One type of regulation that has thus far seemed to work well is safety regulation of US nuclear power plants. A key has been the safety inspection and review by other power plant operators. Recognizing that a problem in one plant by one operator is likely to become a potentially substantive, but certainly public-relations, problem for all, the companies have agreed among themselves to submit to such an inspection by their peers. This promotes the potential spread of best practices. An analogous situation has occurred in the aftermath of the BP Gulf oil spill. A consortium of other Gulf oil operators, led by Exxon, set up an independent, pre-positioned response team and equipment for coordinated rapid response to deal with any future spill. To be sure, this type of "all for one" team approach by the companies themselves only works when the incentives for joint action are strong enough to overcome the companies' individual incentives and protection of competitive proprietary information.

Antitrust regulation is often motivated by fighting monopolies. But potential competition can keep prices down even in an industry with a small number of producers. In some instances, the regulations did more harm than good. Joseph Schumpeter's "creative destruction" idea pointed out that monopoly and monopoly profits eventually beget new technology, competitors, platforms, and methods that undermine the entrenched monopoly and give way to a new one. This serial monopoly is good for innovation and less harmful to consumers than traditionally argued, at least if the new firms come along to provide new options at a rapid enough pace.

These ideas are most important in technology, one of our most innovative sectors. The Federal Communication Commission's attempt to micromanage Internet access is the modern equivalent of the outmoded utility commissions, which ended up eventually stifling and cartelizing their industries.

What was originally called new social regulation—of the environment, for instance, or health and safety—has become ubiquitous in the last few decades. A new set of acronyms—EPA, OSHA, etc.—entered citizens' everyday vocabulary. Some of these regulations made substantial progress on some fronts. But these regulations usually used blunt instruments of command and control, specifying not only goals and targets, but also how these were to be achieved—adding this scrubber, blending that additive, adopting a specific technology. So they came with a large, at least partly unnecessary, cost.

For example, what is certainly on the Top Ten List of the most ridiculous regulations in history occurred when President George W. Bush decided to emphasize cellulosic ethanol in his Advanced Energy Initiative, saying, "Our goal is to make this new kind of ethanol practical and competitive within six years." Cellulosic ethanol was thought to have environmental advantages over corn ethanol. So the Environmental Protection Agency (EPA) required fixed and increasing amounts of it to be blended into motor fuel, toward a target of 1.75 billion gallons.

Energy firms were fined for not blending enough into their fuel. The only problem was that there wasn't much, if any, cellulosic ethanol available. The first attempt to build a plant to meet the EPA's mandates received over $80 million in government subsidies, but closed without ever producing any ethanol. In 2011, the National Academy of Sciences declared it was not possible to produce cellulosic ethanol on a commercial scale with existing technology. A lawsuit resulted in the federal court throwing out the regulation, stating that the "EPA's methodology for making its cellulosic ethanol projection did not take neutral aim at accuracy; it was an unreasonable exercise of agency discretion." The EPA lowered its target by 99 percent. The central failure here was its command that gasoline producers use a fixed quantity of an unproven new fuel, with no regard to price, cost, or feasibility, and no mechanism for adapting to experience.

At the other extreme is the successful Montreal Protocol, a complex international treaty, anchored in sound science, phasing out chemicals depleting atmospheric ozone. A variety of measures have the ozone hole now shrinking. Environmental protection can—and must, in the future—be designed to coexist with strong economic growth.

More recently, laws and regulations have made increasing use of market-based solutions for environmental problems. The two primary mechanisms are tradable permits and Pigovian taxes or subsidies designed to "internalize" social costs (or benefits), such as pollution and congestion, that are generated by economic activity. An important successful example was the emissions trading for sulfur dioxide in the Clean Air Act amendments of 1990. Congestion taxes and time-varying tolls are familiar strategies that are helping to control traffic in many cities around the world, e.g., central London.

Nobel Laureate Ronald Coase taught us that there are strong private incentives to internalize such costs, for example by merger or side payments, when the number of people or firms involved is small. But when the numbers become large, this mechanism breaks down and congestion tolls or emissions charges can, in principle, be designed to improve on the market outcome. However, even market-based solutions can be poorly designed or implemented. Europe's recent carbon-trading program has been highly criticized, for example. If the emissions reductions are too large or too small, getting to the wrong level efficiently may be scant recompense. Or using a market mechanism as a bandage on top of a maze of command and control regulations may convey the impression of efficiency in what is a regulatory cost overrun.

Even scaling down the estimates of costs cited above—and taking a generous interpretation of benefits—leaves an opportunity for huge economic gains from major improvement in the nation's regulatory apparatus. Far more rigorous implementation of unbiased cost-benefit analyses is needed. Currently, most of the analysis of benefits and costs is conducted by the relevant regulatory agency proposing, designing, and overseeing the regulation—when that analysis is done at all. While that agency may have relevant expertise, it may also be captured by the firms it regulates, or its objectivity may be challenged, given its mission and/or political pressures.

To reduce this tendency, the Office of Information and Regulatory Affairs (OIRA) of the OMB has some oversight responsibility for cost-benefit analysis and is supposed, especially, to opine on rules likely to cost in excess of $100 million. While a useful check, it has not proved adequate. In fact, immensely costly regulations have been approved, especially EPA rules, only to be resoundingly overruled by the Supreme Court for failing even to consider costs.

Importantly, there is little *ex post* evaluation of cost estimates, as opposed to *ex ante* prediction. Either OIRA must be substantially beefed up in expertise and independent authority, or an *independent* evaluation body must be authorized to opine between the agencies and the adoption of the rules. In many instances, such review might find more effective and efficient ways to achieve regulatory objectives at less cost to the private sector and, in any event, could expose ludicrously low cost estimates at an early stage.

Greater use of market-based solutions is one promising avenue. A complementary useful tool would be to build conditional "sunsets" into rules at interim periods if they failed to pass *ex post* independent cost-benefit tests based on interim data, thereby forcing corrective action. So long as such a process did not relax *ex ante* scrutiny, it would create incentives for regulatory agencies to design better rules in the first place. And the nature of costs and benefits considered must expand beyond direct costs to the effects of regulation on competition and innovation.

When I was chair of the Council of Economic Advisers, we implemented our own version of this process with the Clean Air Act Amendments of 1990. Concerned that the costs were going to be immense, we got the president to announce that he would veto a bill if costs exceeded a set amount, as estimated by the CEA, not the EPA (as its estimates were controversial). We worked closely with the EPA leadership to implement emissions trading for sulfur dioxide, which *ex post* independent studies estimated reduced compliance costs by 55 percent. Less well known is that I had a signed letter from the EPA administrator agreeing to many other cost-reducing features. These included reasonable implementation of the New Source Review requirement, so firms wouldn't have to do massive upgrades to repair a leaky pipe, and intertemporal trading and banking of the emissions permits. In fact, a futures market in the permits opened before the spot market. While the costs were reduced, *ex post* analysis demonstrated the environmental damage, and the benefits of emission reduction, had been substantially overestimated.

Presidents and Congresses often seek to get around such budgetary or tax constraints that exist by substituting regulation and mandates on the private sector. For example, the regulation and mandates on banks' loans and investments to support low-income housing—instead of raising revenues and providing grants or subsidies directly to borrowers on budget, where costs are harder to hide or ignore and are more likely to be limited—was one of the contributors to the financial crisis and Great Recession.

An overall regulatory budget cap and a requirement stating that an old regulation of comparable cost must be removed for every new regulation imposed—a successful recent reform in Canada— are additional tools to make sure we have effective regulation that balances benefits and costs. Reforms such as these, sensibly implemented, valuable in their own right, can be an important part of a strategy to strengthen growth and opportunity.

CHAPTER 6

NATIONAL AND INTERNATIONAL MONETARY REFORM

John B. Taylor

Sound rules-based monetary policy and good economic performance go hand in hand. In 1776, Adam Smith wrote of the importance of rules for "a well-regulated paper-money" in *The Wealth of Nations*. In 1962, Milton Friedman made the chapter "The Control of Money," with its rationale for monetary rules, a centerpiece of his *Capitalism and Freedom*. Economic research and practical experience in the United States and other countries over the past five decades continue to support this view.

A BRIEF HISTORY OF RULES-BASED POLICY
AND ITS ALTERNATIVES

In the late 1960s and 1970s, the Federal Reserve moved decidedly away from rules-based policy. It became highly discretionary, moving money growth erratically up and down, sometimes flooring the accelerator and other times slamming on the brakes. Yes, the Fed had goals, but it had no consistent strategy to achieve the goals. The result was terrible. Unemployment and inflation both rose.

Then in the early 1980s policy became more systematic and more rules-based, and it stayed that way through the 1990s and into the start of this century. The result was excellent. Inflation and unemployment both came down. Researchers like John Judd and Glenn Rudebusch at the San Francisco Federal Reserve Bank and Richard Clarida, Mark Gertler, and Jordi Gali showed that this improved performance was closely associated with the move to more rules-based policy.[1] They found that the Fed's instrument of policy—the federal funds rate—responded more systematically to developments in the economy. This close connection between policy and performance was just what monetary theory predicted.

Researchers found the same results in other countries. Stephen Cecchetti, Peter Hooper, Bruce Kasman, Kermit Schoenholtz, and Mark Watson showed that as policy became more rule-like in Germany, the United Kingdom, and Japan, economic performance improved.[2] Few complained about international spillovers or beggar-thy-neighbor policies during this period. Sound rules-based monetary policies were not only good for the countries that adopted them, they were good for the international system, too. And again this result is just what monetary theory predicted.

But then a reversal came. The Fed decided to hold the interest rate unusually low during the period from 2003 to 2005, and in doing so it deviated from the rules-based policy that worked well during the 1980s and 1990s. With the inflation rate around 2 percent, the federal funds rate was only 1 percent in 2003, compared with 5.5 percent in 1997 when the inflation rate was also about 2 percent. The results were not good. This policy deviation brought on a search for yield and excesses in the housing market, and was thus a key factor in the financial crisis, especially when combined with a financial regulatory process which broke the rules for safety and soundness.

During the ensuing panic in 2008, the Fed did a good job. It provided liquidity through loans to financial firms and swaps to foreign central banks in a lender-of-last-resort manner. But after the panic the Fed returned to a highly discretionary policy. It initiated its unconventional monetary policy: the large-scale purchases of securities widely known as quantitative easing (QE).

Regardless of what you think of the impact of QE, it was not rule-like or predictable.[3] It did not deliver the economic growth that the Fed forecast and it did not lead to a good recovery. The continuation of the near-zero interest rate was another deviation from rules-based policy.

This deviation from rules-based monetary policy spread to other countries.[4] Central banks followed each other down through extra low interest rates in 2003–2005 and more recently through quantitative easing. QE in the United States was followed by QE in Japan and by QE in the eurozone. Researchers at the Bank for International Settlements called it a Global Great Deviation. Richard Clarida observed that "QE begets QE!" Complaints about spillover and beggar-thy-neighbor policy grew.[5]

This short history demonstrates that shifts toward and away from steady, predictable monetary policy affect economic performance. Alex Nikolsko-Rzhevskyy, David Papell, and Ruxandra Prodan have confirmed these findings using modern econometric tests.[6] In the same journal where their work was published, many other economists (including Michael Bordo, Richard Clarida, John Cochrane, Marvin Goodfriend, Jeffrey Lacker, Allan Meltzer, Lee Ohanian, and Charles Plosser) wrote about the advantages of such a rules-based policy strategy and agreed that during the past decade the Fed has either moved away from a rules-based strategy or has not been clear about what the strategy is.[7]

For all these reasons, any successful blueprint for economic policy should include a sound rules-based monetary policy. Of course, it is possible technically for the Fed to get back to such a policy, but it is difficult in practice. Long departures from a rules-based strategy in the 1970s and in recent years illustrate the difficulty. De jure central bank independence alone as written into the Federal Reserve Act has not prevented departures. De jure central bank independence has been virtually unchanged in the past fifty years, yet policymakers have varied their adherence to rules-based policy.

MONETARY REFORM IN THE UNITED STATES

These variations point to the need for monetary reform legislation to require the Fed to adopt a rules-based monetary strategy or rule. I offered such a proposal several years ago,[8] which would effectively restore and modernize reporting and accountability requirements for the instruments of monetary policy in the Federal Reserve Act.

A proposal along these lines has now been written into legislation. Section 2 of the Fed Oversight Reform and Modernization Act is entitled "Requirements for Policy Rules of the Federal Open Market Committee." It would require the Fed to "describe the strategy or rule of the Federal Open Market Committee for the systematic quantitative adjustment" of its policy instruments. The act, which passed the House of Representatives on November 19, 2015, would simply require that the Fed choose a strategy and decide how to describe it. The Fed could change its strategy or deviate from it if circumstances called for a change, in which case the Fed would have to explain why.

Policy rules legislation with similar provisions was voted out of the Senate Committee on Banking, Housing, and Urban Affairs in 2015, so working out a compromise with the House legislation in conference should be feasible. If such a bill passed Congress and were signed into law, it would constitute the needed reform of the Federal Reserve Act.

In evaluating such legislation, it is important to emphasize the word "strategy" as explicitly stated in the legislation. Though economists frequently use the word "rule," that term may convey the false idea that a rules-based monetary strategy must be purely mechanical. George Shultz explained the importance of having a strategy. He wrote that "it is important, based on my own experience, to have a rules-based monetary policy. . . . At least as I have observed from policy decisions over the years in various fields, if you have a strategy, you get somewhere. If you don't have a strategy, you are just a tactician at large and it doesn't add up." Fed Chair Janet Yellen similarly explained in a speech in the 1990s that "the existence of policy tradeoffs requires a strategy for managing them" and she showed how a rule for the policy instruments could serve as "a general strategy for conducting monetary policy."

The United States Congress has responsibility for the oversight of monetary policy in this strategic sense. As Allan Meltzer recently testified,[9] "We need change to improve the oversight that [Congress] . . . exercises over the Fed. . . . You need a rule which says, look, you said you were going to do this, and you have not done it. That requires an answer, and that I think is one of the most important reasons why we need some kind of a rule."

There is precedent for this type of congressional oversight. Legislation that appeared in the Federal Reserve Act from 1977 to 2000 required reporting of the ranges of the monetary aggregates. The legislation did not specify exactly what the numerical settings of these ranges should be, but the greater focus on the money and credit ranges was helpful in the disinflation efforts of the 1980s. When the requirement for reporting ranges for the monetary aggregates was removed from the law in 2000, nothing was put in its place. A legislative void was thus created concerning reporting requirements and accountability. The proposed legislative reform would help fill that void.

There has been extensive discussion and debate in the Congress and in the media about the ideas underlying this type of legislation, and new economic research has begun to address the issue.[10] Recently a number of economists—including Nobel Prize winners, former Fed officials, and monetary experts—signed a statement in support of the legislation. The statement is attached as an appendix to this essay.

There is currently opposition to the legislation from the Federal Reserve. Fed Chair Janet Yellen testified,[11] "I don't believe that the Fed should chain itself to any mechanical rule." But the bill does not chain the Fed to any rule. The Fed would choose and describe its own strategy, and it need not be mechanical. The Fed could change the strategy if the world changed. It could deviate from the strategy in a crisis if it explained why. It would still serve as lender of last resort or take appropriate actions in the event of a crisis. Moreover, a policy strategy or rule does not require that any instrument of policy be fixed, but rather that it flexibly adjust up or down to economic developments in a systematic and predictable way that can be explained.

Another stated concern with policy rules legislation is that the Fed would lose its independence. In my view, based on my own experience in government and my research, the opposite is more likely. A clear public strategy helps prevent policymakers from bending under pressure and sacrificing their institution's independence.

Some commentators say that the reform would require the Fed to follow a particular rule listed in the bill, but this is not the case. The bill requires the Fed to describe how its strategy or rule might differ from a "reference rule," which happens to be the Taylor rule. However, describing the difference between a policy rule and this reference rule is a natural and routine task for the Fed. In fact, many at the Fed (including Yellen) already make such comparisons.

Another critique is that the zero bound on the interest rate means that an interest rate rule is no longer useful. Wasn't that the reason that the Fed deviated from rules-based policy in recent years? It was certainly not a reason in 2003–2005 and it is not a reason now, because the zero bound is not binding. It appears that there was a short period in 2009 when zero was clearly binding. But the zero bound is not a new thing in economics research. Policy rule design research took that into account long ago.[12] One approach was to recognize that in such a situation one should simply keep money growth steady rather than embarking on a purely discretionary policy such as quantitative easing.

There is also the concern that there are many rules or strategies to choose from. There are many different types of personal display devices, but that doesn't mean they are all useless. Some policy strategies are better than others, and it makes perfect sense for researchers and policymakers to be looking for new and better ones. Some people have suggested focusing on nominal GDP. I do not think adding housing prices or the stock market to a rule makes much sense, but with the policy rules legislation it is the job of the Fed to decide.

Some of the recent objections to predictable policy rules and the enabling legislation go to the heart of an old debate about rules versus discretion. Lawrence Summers raised this one: "I think about my doctor. Which would I prefer: for my doctor's advice to be consistently predictable or for my doctor's advice to be responsive to the medical condition with which I present? Me, I'd rather have a doctor who most of the time didn't tell me to take some stuff, and every once in a while said I needed to ingest some stuff into my body in response to the particular problem that I had. That would be a doctor whose [advice], believe me, would be less predictable."[13]

This line of argument in favor of pure discretion appeals to an all-knowing expert, a doctor who does not perceive the need for, and does not use, a set of guidelines, but who once in a while in an unpredictable way says to ingest some stuff. But as in economics, there has been progress in medicine over the years. And much progress has been due to doctors using checklists. Experience shows that checklists are invaluable for preventing mistakes and for getting good diagnoses and appropriate treatments.[14] Of course doctors need to exercise judgement in implementing checklists, but if they start winging it or skipping steps the patients usually suffer. Experience and empirical studies show that checklist-free medicine is fraught with dangers just as is a rules-free monetary policy.

Another line of argument is that you do not really need a rule or strategy for the instruments of policy. All you really need for effective policymaking is a goal, such as an inflation target and an employment target. In medicine, it would be the goal of a healthy patient. The rest of policymaking is doing whatever you as an expert, or you as an expert with models, think needs to be done with the instruments. You do not need to articulate or describe a strategy, a decision rule, or a contingency plan for the instruments. If you want to hold the interest rate well below the rule-based strategy that worked well during the Great Moderation, as the Fed did in 2003–2005, then it's OK as long as you can justify it at the moment in terms of the goal.

Ben Bernanke and others have called this approach "constrained discretion."[15] It is an appealing term, and it may be constraining discretion in some sense, but it is not inducing or encouraging a rule or a strategy. Simply having a specific numerical goal is not a rule for the instruments of policy; it is not a strategy. In my view, it ends up being all tactics. I think the evidence shows that relying solely on constrained discretion has not worked for monetary policy.

INTERNATIONAL MONETARY REFORM

As I discussed in the "brief history" earlier in this essay, the international monetary system has also drifted away in recent years from the kind of steady, rules-based system long advocated by monetary economists and practitioners from Milton Friedman to Paul Volcker. The deviations from rule-based monetary policy seem to spread from country to country. Because these deviations cause movements in exchange rates, they are also causing governments to impose capital controls, intervene in exchange markets, and use regulations to affect international exchange transactions. The international financial institutions are even endorsing such controls, a clear contrast with the 1990s when they were working to remove them.[16]

The resulting international economic performance has been poor. There are huge swings of capital flows into and out of emerging markets, increased volatility of exchange rates, and disappointing economic growth in many emerging markets and developing countries.

In my view, the problem traces to deviations from rules-based monetary policies at the national level. Bouts of quantitative easing (QE) have been associated with large fluctuations in exchange rates akin to currency wars. As QE in the United States begets QE in Japan which in turn begets QE in Europe, exchange rates move sharply in each instance. Interest rate decisions at central banks also tend to spread around the world and also resemble currency wars. Central banks have tended to follow each other. Extra low interest rates in the United States were followed by extra low interest rates in many other countries, in an effort to fight off currency appreciations. Their action in turn has led to interest rates being lower than otherwise in the United States.

We need a new international strategy to deal with these problems. Any strategy should be based on the principle that a key foundation of a rules-based international monetary system is simply a rules-based monetary policy in each country. Thus one proposal would be for the United States to work with other countries to forge an agreement where each country commits to a rules-based monetary strategy. It would be a flexible exchange rate system in which each country—each central bank—describes and commits to a monetary policy rule or strategy for setting the policy instruments. The strategy could include a specific inflation target and some notion of the long-run interest rate, as well as a list of key variables to react to in certain ways. It would be the job of each central bank to formulate and describe its strategy. The strategies could be changed if the world changed or if there were an emergency. A procedure for describing the change and the reasons for it would be in the agreement.

For the new agreement to work well, it should include a commitment to remove capital controls eventually. This would be a difficult part of the reform: currently, there are sixty-four countries, including China, classified as "wall" or "gate" countries with varying degrees of capital controls. For this reason, a transition period would be needed.

There's an important lesson from previous international monetary agreements that this proposal must also take account of. Consider the Plaza Accord of the 1980s, which included the United States, the United Kingdom, Japan, Germany, and France. Under the Plaza Accord, the Bank of Japan agreed to shift its monetary policy in a way that adversely affected its economy—too tight at first and too easy later—causing a severe boom and bust. In contrast, US monetary policy was not affected: the Fed simply clarified in a constructive way what it was already doing, and the US economy performed well. The lesson is that any agreement should not impose specific strategies on central banks, except to say that the strategies be reported. Such a process would pose no threat to the national or international independence of central banks.

Now is a good time for such an international reform. Paul Volcker and Jaime Caruana, the head of the Bank for International Settlements, and others have been calling for reform. Nevertheless, reform will be difficult because there is still disagreement about the diagnosis and the remedy as proposed here. Moreover, some countries are still in the midst of unconventional discretionary monetary policies, and even if they move toward a rules-based policy there is a question of follow-through and commitment.

In my view, such an international monetary reform will require strong US leadership. In this regard, there is an important link between the US reform proposal and the international reform proposal in this essay. US leadership would be bolstered if the Congress became a partner in the international agreement by passing legislation requiring that the Fed report and commit to a monetary policy strategy as in the Fed Oversight Reform and Modernization Act.

CONCLUSION

The national and international monetary reform proposals in this essay may not be the be-all and end-all, but they are supported by lessons learned from economic history and extensive research over the years. A reform by which the Federal Reserve commits to a rule-based strategy, and clearly explains temporary deviations from that strategy, would create a more transparent and predictable process with accountability. It would meet Milton Friedman's goal of "legislating rules for the conduct of monetary policy that will have the effect of enabling the public to exercise control over monetary policy through its political authorities, while at the same time . . . prevent[ing] monetary policy from being subject to the day-by-day whim of political authorities."[17] And on the international side, each country could choose its own independent monetary strategy, avoid interfering with the principles of free and open markets, and contribute to the common good of global stability and growth.[18]

Economists' Statement on Policy Rules Legislation

We support the legislation entitled Requirements for Policy Rules of the Federal Open Market Committee, Section 2 of the Fed Oversight Reform and Modernization Act (H.R. 3189) which passed the House of Representatives on November 19, 2015. This important reform would lead to more predictable rules-based monetary policy. It is based on evidence and experience that monetary policy works best when it follows a clear, predictable rule or strategy. A rule reduces uncertainty by giving the public information about future policy actions.

The legislation requires that the Fed "describe the strategy or rule of the Federal Open Market Committee for the systematic quantitative adjustment" of its policy instruments. The Fed would choose the strategy and how to describe it. The legislation does not chain the Fed to any rule, and certainly not to a mechanical rule. The Fed could change its strategy or deviate from it if circumstances called for a change, in which case the Fed would have to explain why. To improve communication about its strategy, the legislation requires that the Fed compare its rule or strategy with a reference rule, as is common practice.

The legislation enables the Congress to exercise better oversight over monetary policy. It would prevent the Congress from micromanaging the Fed or subjecting it to capricious short-run changes in political views or desires. If the Fed says that it plans to follow a strategy and it does not, then an answer is required. There is precedent for this type of oversight: from 1977 to 2000 the Federal Reserve Act required that the Fed set and report ranges of the monetary aggregates. The new legislation would fill a void created by repeal of that oversight in 2000.

The Fed would still serve as lender of last resort or take appropriate actions in the event of a crisis. Having a strategy or rule does not mean that instruments of policy are fixed, but rather that they adjust in a systematic and predictable way.

In no way would the legislation compromise the Fed's independence. On the contrary, publically reporting a strategy helps prevent policy makers from bending under pressure and sacrificing independence. It strengthens independence by reducing or removing pressures from markets and governments to finance budget deficits or deviate from policies that enhance economic stability.

The decision by the Fed to adopt a numerical inflation goal is welcome, but such a goal is not a strategy for the instruments of policy. The new legislation would provide for that strategy, and thereby improve economic performance.

Lars Peter Hansen, Robert Lucas, Edward Prescott,
George Shultz, Robert Heller, Jerry Jordan, Athanasios
Orphanides, William Poole, Michael Bordo, Michael Boskin,
Charles Calomiris, Varadarajan Chari, John Cochrane, John
Cogan, Steven Davis, Marvin Goodfriend, Gregory Hess,
Peter Ireland, Mickey Levy, Bennett McCallum, Allan Meltzer,
Gerald O'Driscoll, Lee Ohanian, Scott Sumner, John Taylor

CHAPTER 7

A BLUEPRINT FOR EFFECTIVE FINANCIAL REFORM

John H. Cochrane

The most recent financial regulatory expansion, under the Dodd-Frank Act in the United States and similar actions by foreign countries and international organizations, is a failure. It is leading to a sclerotic, inefficient, and politicized financial system. Most of all, it won't work, neither stopping a new crisis from emerging nor stopping another round of bailouts if a crisis does occur.[1]

Rather than stress these failures, which many eloquent authors have done, I focus here on the essential question: *What is the alternative?*

A VISION

Let us start with a vision of what a healthy financial system looks like. Then, we can consider policy paths to take us there.

We want a financial system that is immune from crises. We also want an innovative, competitive financial system, one that brings all the advantages that the revolutions in computation, communication, and finance can bring to savers and investors.

As much as possible, we want to minimize government direc-

I thank John Cogan, Chris Dauer, and Michael Boskin for very helpful comments.

tion of the financial system. Where regulation is necessary, we want it to operate by clear, simple laws and rules, not by the discretionary decisions of powerful agencies and by tens of thousands of pages of inscrutable regulations. Limited rule-based regulation is not necessarily a goal in itself; instead, it springs from long experience that vast and powerful regulatory bureaucracies do not produce innovative, competitive, and apolitical financial systems, a better allocation of investment capital, less risk-taking, or immunity from crises.

On the other hand, given our government's irresistible temptation to meddle, especially where large amounts of money are involved, we want a financial system that is resistant to such meddling, one for which regulation and cross-subsidization will not induce financial instability as our previous regulatory regime so obviously did.

What would a structure that embodies these goals look like?

Equity-financed banking

First, and most importantly: banks and similar financial institutions will get their money almost entirely by selling stock or by retaining earnings—rather than paying earnings out as dividends —and by long-term borrowing. They will not be funded by large amounts of short-term debt. (Retained earnings raise the value of current shares, so selling stock and retaining earnings are the same thing.)

Financial crises are runs, no more and no less. A run occurs when creditors such as depositors or overnight lenders, unsure of a bank's long-run prospects, demand their money immediately, each anxious to be repaid first. When the bank cannot borrow elsewhere, issue equity, sell assets, or otherwise raise cash to fulfill its promises to such creditors, the bank fails. A crisis is a systemic run: simultaneous runs on many related banks or similar financial institutions.

If we can engineer a run-free financial system, we stop financial

crises and we achieve the most important goal of financial regulation. Much additional regulation would no longer be needed. Ill-
advised regulation, cronyism, protection, and capture will likely
continue anyway. But without financial crises, their damage will
be sharply reduced.

Equity-financed banking stops runs, and a financial system of
such institutions is immune from crises. Consider the extreme
case: a bank that gets all its money by issuing equity, and uses that
money to make loans. Such a bank simply cannot fail. Yes, it may
lose money and customers, its shareholders may lose the value of
their investments, and the firm may eventually close, sell, or liq-
uidate. But financial "failure" means failure to pay debts or other
fixed promises. If a firm has no debt, it cannot fail to pay debt; it
cannot go bankrupt.

A stock price decline is not a financial crisis. When stocks lose
value, the stock investors cannot demand their money back from
the company; they cannot seize assets or take the company to
bankruptcy court; they cannot run. They can demand management changes. They can, individually, sell shares. They can, col-
lectively, drive share prices down. Their desire to sell may even
be "irrational" and subject to behavioral biases including herd-
ing, waves of optimism and pessimism, and so forth. Stock prices
may be irrationally volatile or bubbly. But none of this constitutes
a financial crisis. In no case is money promised and not delivered. In no case does the economy come to a standstill of broken
promises to deliver nonexistent cash. Nobody goes to bankruptcy court. Companies may ignore stock prices and continue
operations.

Stock price crashes are only dangerous if investors or banks
have borrowed a lot of money to buy stocks. Then, the stock price
crash causes debts to fail. But debt is at fault here, not the stock
market.

Long-term debt may cause a failure, if a company cannot make
a scheduled interest or principal payment. But long-term bond-

holders or lenders (certificates of deposit, for example) do not have the right to demand their money immediately. If the value of a company's assets falls, or the assets become illiquid so nobody really knows what they are worth, long-term bondholders, like stockholders, see the resale value of their investment shrink, possibly temporarily; but there is nothing they can do about it right away either. Long-term debt is not quite as good as common equity for preventing crises, but it is a lot better than short-term debt.

We do not need to regulate this level of perfection. An institution that is funded 95 percent by equity and long-term debt is so unlikely to suffer a run that it is for all intents and purposes completely safe.

Second: short-term, run-prone financing will be absent. Short-term debt is the poison in the well. Our crisis-free economy will treat it as such.

Investors will transparently bear risks, rather than pretend that each can get out first with full value and that risk has somehow been "transformed" or magically wished away. Banks and similar financial institutions will not fund the bulk of their investments with overnight debt, interbank lending, short-term commercial paper, or other wholesale, very short-term financing, all of which suffered runs in 2008.

Short-term debt is the means by which problems at one firm spread to the rest of the system. When Lehman Brothers failed, it was leveraged thirty to one overnight. For each dollar of capital, each morning, it had to borrow 30 new dollars to pay off 30 dollars borrowed the previous evening. That this system fell apart should not be much of a surprise. That our regulatory effort concentrates on regulators overseeing the safety of such firms' investments, rather than eliminating this obviously run-prone means of financing investments, is the surprise.

I emphasize the absence of short-term "financing." Companies do, and must, engage in lots of short-term or fixed-payment contracts, including receivables, trade credit, and derivatives. But, first, many such contracts do not have the feature that the counterparty can demand repayment at any time and put the company into bankruptcy if not paid; and, second, such contracts are usually matched by offsetting assets so the firm has little net short-term exposure and a large equity cushion. The danger lies when firms finance a risky asset position with a large net amount of short-term, instantly demandable debt, whose failure to pay triggers bankruptcy.

Mortgages will still be bundled into mortgage-backed securities, hopefully without Fannie Mae and Freddie Mac and government guarantees. But mortgage-backed securities will be held in long-only mutual and exchange traded funds, by pension funds, insurance companies, endowments, by everyday investors in retirement accounts, and even by equity-financed banks. Mortgage-backed securities are not particularly risky—they are far safer than most corporate equity.

But mortgage-backed securities will not be funded by constantly rolled-over short-term borrowing in a bank or in "shadow banks" such as auction-rate securities or special-purpose vehicles with off-balance-sheet bank guarantees. Then, when the market value or liquidity of mortgage-backed securities declines, even temporarily (as it turned out in many cases), you and I suffer small mark-to-market losses on our investment portfolios. Panicked investors may sell to others at a loss. Others step in to make fortunes buying when others panic—your "fire sale" is my "buying opportunity." But nobody can demand their money back immediately, so the issuing institutions do not fail, and the financial world does not end.

Deposits and payments

With no fixed-value, immediately demandable deposits, where will people put their money, and where will money for loans come from? The broad answer is that this financial system can provide the same or better menu of assets to savers, and as much or more credit and investment capital to businesses and homebuyers, as our current one does.

Those wishing to have immediately available, completely liquid, fixed-value investments will still have them. Banks may still offer deposits and checking accounts. However, such liabilities must be backed 100 percent by short-term Treasuries or interest-paying reserves, in ways that are completely insulated from bankruptcy of the parent company. For example, banks could set up money market funds that hold interest-paying reserves or short-term Treasuries. Deposits and withdrawals at an ATM machine are simply bank-managed purchases and sales of such funds.

To accommodate this demand, the Fed could keep its large balance sheet of Treasury securities and allow individuals and non-bank businesses to have interest-paying accounts. Better, in my view, the Treasury could offer fixed-value floating-rate debt, with cheap electronic transfers, reserves for everyone. If people do not hold these securities directly, they can hold funds that in turn hold these securities.[2]

Deposits backed by short-term Treasuries or reserves can't fail. This fact can substitute for today's deposit insurance. More importantly, it can substitute for the Federal Deposit Insurance Corporation's resolution mechanism, which promptly takes over banks at the FDIC's discretion, and the ominous Dodd-Frank resolution authority. More importantly still, large depositors are not currently protected by deposit insurance and have turned to "shadow banking" of overnight but run-prone debt as a result. Deposits consisting of, or backed 100 percent by, reserves or Treasury debt can completely substitute for these demands.

We are actually on the way to this vision now. The Treasury has introduced floating-rate debt whose value fluctuates very little. The Federal Reserve pays interest on bank reserves, and its enormous balance sheet implies that we now have about $2 trillion of narrow banking—$2 trillion of bank deposits that are backed by interest-paying Fed reserves. The Fed has also introduced segregated accounts and reverse repurchase agreements, which allow large depositors to invest in interest-paying reserves.

However, though consumers and businesses can choose to hold the same assets as they have today, they are likely to choose differently. In today's financial system, and more so in the future, transactions services and liquidity no longer require fixed-value, run-prone accounts. You could easily make purchases with a credit card, debit card, or cell phone and pay the bill by selling shares of a floating-value stock fund, bond fund, mortgage-backed security, or shares of bank stock. In the 1930s, or even the 1960s, this was not possible. Buying and selling assets took large commissions, bid-ask spreads, and days of time to clear. People had to park a considerable amount of wealth in low-yielding, fixed-value investments in order to make payments. Now, people who want greater returns than short-term Treasury debt or Fed reserves offer, but who need liquid assets to pay bills, can do both by taking on some price risk. Given the option, they may choose to do so, and the large amounts of short-term, run-prone securities held for transactions purposes may evaporate. Banks may even offer products that look much like savings accounts—except that, like all proper long-term debt, the face value fluctuates over time.

What investors will not have are accounts that promise fixed values and instant withdrawals, but generate high yields by investing in risky private securities. If savers want higher interest rates than are offered on short-term Treasury securities, they will shoulder price risks rather than demand full value back from the issuer.

Equity-financed banks will not lack for funds to lend out. The same flow of savings ends up in the same amount of loans and government debt. Investors and taxpayers need not provide the banks any more funds than they do now, and need not shoulder any more risk. The equity of an unleveraged bank would have very low volatility, roughly the volatility of the banks' combined debt and equity now. The same Treasuries that the private sector holds directly will be held via intermediaries, or in fixed-value form.

REGULATION AND DEREGULATION

How do we get there?

Before one proposes a wave of new regulations, it is wise to remove the unintended consequences of the old regulations that push the system away from this vision.

Debt deductibility

Short-term debt financing is the poison in the well, and equity financing cures crises. Yet companies can deduct interest payments against income, but not dividend payments. Our government subsidizes debt and simultaneously tries to regulate against its use. Removing this distortion is a good first step.

Abolishing the corporate tax is the purest solution. But we don't have to be that pure. At a minimum, dividend payments and interest should be treated equally, either allowing the deductibility of the latter or denying it to the former.

Other debt subsidies

Liquidity regulations are an underappreciated incentive to unstable financing. A wide swath of financial regulations prizes short-term debt as an *asset*. In doing so, they create a large market and lower interest rates, which gives other firms incentives to create lots of long-term debt as a *liability*.

Among others, Fed liquidity regulations tell banks to hold lots of short-term debt. Securities and Exchange Commission regulations tell mutual funds to hold short-term debt. Capital regulations and the Fed's stress tests use low risk-weights for short-term debt held as an asset.

Regulations that prize holding liquid assets are particularly ill-conceived. Banks plan to sell assets to raise cash if their creditors want money back. That may work in normal times. But who is going to buy assets in a crisis? The whole point of post-Dodd-Frank financial regulation is supposed to be to protect the financial *system* against *systemic* runs.

The regulators' attitude toward any short-term debt other than Treasuries should be that the purchaser is gambling that it can run first; the *lender* is as much a contributor to systemic runs as the borrower.

Deposit insurance and the wider anticipation of *ex-post* creditor guarantees are additional inducements to issue and to buy too much debt. It is easy to say that the government really, really will not bail out creditors next time they run. But that promise has been proven false time and again. Ringing just as hollow is the idea that Dodd-Frank resolution authority will impose haircuts, in a crisis, on creditors who will be screaming that the world will end if they lose money. Once the run has started, creditor guarantees are the only way to stop it, and moral hazard worriers in a crisis are as rare as the proverbial atheists in foxholes.

It is better to restructure the financial system so that runs don't happen and creditor guarantees are not needed. In the Dodd-Frank fantasy world, this happens because wise regulators stop over-leveraged institutions from ever losing money again. In this proposal, the absence of run-prone debt means that inevitable losses do not spark a panic or the need for bailouts.

Regulatory safe harbor

In the current regulatory system there is no safe harbor. There is no way a financial company can certify, "We have set up our business as you ask; we do not pose a systemic risk. Leave us alone." Even equity asset managers, who manage clients' money directly, are now being considered for "systemic" designation under the theory that they might drive stock prices down from irrational behavior.

The carrot is better than the stick. Rather than add regulations against short-term debt, we can grant regulatory safe harbor to institutions that don't use it. If a bank or other institution has a large level of capital—say 50 percent equity capital and no more than 20 percent short-term debt—then it can be automatically free from large swaths of asset risk regulation. Do what you want, as you cannot fail and cause a problem.

The current regulatory philosophy, and especially its Dodd-Frank epitome, is curiously silent on this vision thing. What is not, and cannot, be systemic? How can a financial institution structure itself so that it is so patently safe that it needs no regulation? The loud silence to these questions betrays the answer: the authors of our financial regulations do not think any financial arrangement can be conducted privately, without detailed regulatory scrutiny. We will not escape financial sclerosis with repeated crises without *some* vision for private finance safe enough not to need lots of regulation.

A debt tax

Even without subsidies, bailout guarantees, and regulatory incentives, financial companies may choose to issue too much short-term debt. We need good tools to actively discourage it.

Capital ratios are the centerpiece of current debt regulation. The trouble with these is that attention moves from the numerator to the denominator: 20 percent capital, maybe, but 20 percent of what? Currently, the answer is "risk-weighted assets." Risk-weights pose obvious problems and engender obvious games. Greek government debt still counts for essentially no risk-weight on European bank balance sheets. Mortgage-backed securities gave lower regulatory risk-weight than their equivalent portfolio of individual loans, so banks preferred the securities to the loans. Risk-weights are fundamentally mistaken, treating risks on an asset-by-asset, rather than a portfolio, basis. But raw leverage-ratio limits, ignoring the riskiness of assets, are just as perverse.

A tax on debt, with a higher tax on short-term debt, is a better way to induce firms to rely more on long-term debt and equity and to avoid risk-weight games. For each dollar of short-term borrowing, a financial institution might pay two cents per year. Each dollar of long-term borrowing (no principal payments for a year, say), would cost one cent per year.

This form of policy would give a strong incentive to reduce short-term debt, without the complexity or games involved in regulatory capital ratios. Conversely, if debt really is as vital as banks say it is when they're fighting regulators, well, then they should still be able to issue it and pay the tax.

The principle is the same as a pollution tax. Short-term debt poses an externality. It offers the option to run, and if one person runs he imposes losses on other investors. So, if you want to pollute markets with run-prone debt, pay a hefty tax to do so.

Accounting and tax reform

Arbitrary accounting and tax conventions also drive our financial system to include too much run-prone short-term debt. Short-term debt held as an asset counts as "cash" on the balance sheet, making no distinction between run-free cash (bills, Treasuries, money market funds backed by Treasuries) and run-prone short-term debt.

Accounting and tax rules keep floating-value accounts from being used for transactions, though such use is now easy given the speed of current financial transactions. If one holds a mutual fund with slightly floating values, then each transaction at slightly different prices triggers short-term capital gains and losses. These are, at a minimum, an accounting headache, and at maximum a significant drag.

These conventions need to be reformed, and it would not be too costly to do so. Even if we don't do the right thing by removing the capital gains tax entirely, floating-value accounts used for transactions can be exempt from a tax aimed at "speculators." The effort is tiny compared to the cost of financial crises or Dodd-Frank regulations.

Finally, regulation

If removing the many subsidies for short-term debt, removing the regulatory, accounting, and tax preferences for short-term debt, allowing a regulatory safe-harbor for run-proof institutions, and adding a simple tax on short-term debt do not together convert the financial system to one in which short-term debt is rare, and most institutions are financed by run-proof floating-value assets, then yes, one could add regulation. Capital standards like the ones in place now can be stiffened substantially. One could also avoid the risk-weight game by regulating the ratio of debt to market value of equity, rather than the ratio of debt to dubious measures of risk-weighted assets.

And deregulation

The key point: once run-prone liabilities are sharply reduced, and the financial system is free of the danger of crises and runs, the vast structure of asset risk regulation can be repealed or simply allowed to die on the vine. It does not matter to financial stability how a bank invests its money if losses at that bank do not cause the seizing up of a systemic run. No more stress tests, no more thousands of pages of Basel rules, no more detailed micro-management by Fed staffers embedded in big banks—and no more creditor or bank bailouts. They simply won't be needed.

The Fed is moving this way of its own accord. It is gradually requiring once unthinkable levels of capital—through levels of capital common in the pre-regulation era—and placing less and less faith in its own clairvoyant abilities to spot the next crisis coming and tell the banks how to invest to avoid losing money in the first place.

CAVEAT

This is, in many ways, a conservative outline of monetary and financial reform.

Much else needs fixing, of course, including getting rid of Fannie and Freddie, the absurd over-regulation of institutions and markets, the witch hunt for billion-dollar settlements, the alphabet soup of regulatory agencies, the SEC, CFTC, CFPB, OCC, and so forth. A full reform proposal deconstructs this whole spaghetti tangle.

This proposal is, though, the necessary first step. "Financial stability" is the mantra under which a blanket of regulation has fallen over our markets and institutions. Once that genuine problem is solved, the rest of the blanket can be attacked. Likewise, if we can solve the one central problem of crises, then remaining bad financial regulation becomes a simple drag on the economy, just like many other regulations, not a crisis-provoker.

This proposal is conservative in another way. The monetary system I describe remains based on short-term government debt as the basic foundation of money and financial transactions. (Currency and reserves at the Fed are just short-term government debt.) I steer away from bitcoin, gold, private money, free banking, and related proposals.

Our financial system has evolved to this basic structure. With inflation near zero and demand for US government debt unprecedentedly solid, there would be little consensus for changing it. And while such a change may be desirable in the long run, it is not necessary for stopping private financial crises like the one we just experienced.

However, as a result, the system I outline requires that the United States retain a strong fiscal position so that its short-term debt is unquestionably safe. The United States could inflate, and it could even default on long-term debts. But our financial system currently, and under this proposal, requires complete faith that the United States would never default on its short-term debts.

Designing a financial system robust to sovereign default—not just defaults in private assets such as mortgage-backed securities—is an interesting challenge. If we do not get our fiscal house in order, as many of the accompanying essays stress, it is a challenge we may face sooner rather than later. But insulating the financial system from sovereign default can come second, and later. First, get rid of private, run-inducing short-term financing; and second, create better underlying money. And thinking about this issue at the end of a long road should not derail adoption of the straightforward, though fundamental, steps needed to overcome our current, enormous, and failed financial regulatory regime.

OUR NATIONAL HUMAN RESOURCES

George P. Shultz

An examination of demographic trends and educational developments puts a sharp focus on the urgent need to improve K-12 education, as well as on immigration policy, if the United States is to have a healthy and expanding economy. Remember, economic expansion comes fundamentally from expansion in the labor force with an increasing productivity of that labor force. The chapters that follow delve into each of these issues, but here again I'll just set the agenda. So let's start with demography.

In the years from 2010 to 2030, there will be no change in the number of people age forty-five to sixty-four. In the twenty to forty-four age group, the increase will be very small. Instead, the big increase will come in the group of those age sixty-five and up. The population is aging rapidly, and the cohort in the prime labor force years is not increasing. Meanwhile, the proportion of the population sixteen years of age and older who are in the labor force has already declined sharply in recent years, going down from 66 percent in early 2007 to about 62.9 percent today, probably the result of poor economic policies.

The problem of having a capable labor force is heightened by the fact that, at this time, 35 percent of Hispanics, a rapidly rising share of the population, have not even finished high school. Plenty of evidence and experience show that good educational outcomes are possible. The United States need not be falling behind.

Give students a real choice on which school to attend, so schools must compete for students. With reasonable administrative control, a better-educated labor force will emerge.

As we aim to improve the capacities of our younger workers, an additional important policy program will be to seek ways to keep people in the labor force for longer. Labor force participation by people sixty-five and older is encouraging, as are attitudes. Surveys show that many employers consider older workers as being sometimes more productive than younger workers. Policy changes can help. As an example, the payroll tax could be eliminated once a worker reaches the age of eligibility for full benefits, currently about to rise to sixty-seven. That would mean that older workers would have more take-home pay and would be less expensive to employ.

As we work around these issues of the size of the labor force, we can also take separate steps to help keep up its scaler in productivity.

For example, the productivity issue underscores the importance of research and development, which has always been, and continues to be, a companion to our country's creative and innovative culture. We need to encourage innovation in the private sector and beef up R&D support from the federal government. Experience shows that a serious federal program—long-term in vision, sustained year-to-year, and credible in its aims—will be joined by significant private funds, which want to know what is being developed and how to contribute.

We can also think about how to change our immigration system so that greater emphasis is put on the potential productivity of those who come to our shores. That means less emphasis on extended families (uncles, cousins, etc.) and more emphasis on skills and education, including a virtually automatic green card to those educated in the United States. So we need to bring in people of working age who are well-educated and can contribute to the economic expansion that will be needed if we are going to cope successfully with the big growth in the number of retirees.

Immigration is a sensitive issue for many people. But it is an understatement to point out that this is not the first time our country has wrestled with the topic. In a speech he gave at the White House in 1989, Ronald Reagan chose to reflect on its special standing when he told us:

> Yes, the torch of Lady Liberty symbolizes our freedom and represents our heritage, the compact with our parents, our grandparents, and our ancestors. Other countries may seek to compete with us; but in one vital area, as a beacon of freedom and opportunity that draws the people of the world, no country on Earth comes close. This, I believe, is one of the most important sources of America's greatness. We lead the world because, unique among nations, we draw our people—our strength—from every country and every corner of the world. And by doing so, we continuously renew and enrich our nation. While other countries cling to the stale past, here in America we breathe life into dreams. We create the future, and the world follows us into tomorrow. Thanks to each wave of new arrivals to this land of opportunity, we're a nation forever young, forever bursting with energy and new ideas, and always on the cutting edge, always leading the world to the new frontier. This quality is vital to our future as a nation. If we ever closed the door to new Americans, our leadership in the world would soon be lost.

The need to reform our immigration system is widely recognized, but constructive efforts seem to be hung up on the issue of "securing the borders." In my view, that problem could be more effectively addressed if we took more time to understand it. For example, the problem appears to be our border with Mexico, but, with Mexican fertility rates falling to slightly below the replacement level and the Mexican economy improving, net immigration of Mexicans to the United States has been zero in recent years. The more relevant problem is therefore Mexico's southern border. We need to ask how we can help Mexico avoid becoming a transit country with all of the human degradation and corruption that go with it.

In sum, our human resource base can be adequate and productive. We simply need to do those things that are obviously needed and that we have demonstrated that we know how to do. An expanding economy will pull people back into the labor force; applying the principles of choice and competition in K-12 education will help high school graduation rates and continuing college attendance; simple reforms can keep people productive in their more senior years; and informed work on immigration can encourage the flow of "the best and the brightest" to our shores.

CHAPTER 8

EDUCATION AND
THE NATION'S FUTURE

Eric A. Hanushek

The quality of schools in the United States has received constant federal attention since the 1957 launch of Sputnik, America's first major intellectual scare. Pronouncements, commissions, and legislation have all followed at fairly regular intervals since then, and scarcely anyone argues that we are in a good place with education. Yet evidence of improvement is hard to find. In simplest terms, the future of the United States is closely related to the education of its population, and the nation requires strong leadership to move it to a better position.

This essay reviews the current state of American education and discusses why it is important. The main focus is K-12 education, where the largest concerns rest; but there is attention given to specifics elsewhere. It then considers alternative policy approaches and the role of the federal government.

WHERE THE UNITED STATES STANDS

Historically, the United States outpaced the rest of the world in terms of human capital. The United States introduced universal secondary schooling before other developed countries. But today the United States has below-average secondary school completion rates among OECD (Organisation for Economic Co-operation and Development) countries.

More importantly, achievement of US students lags behind students in a large number of countries. There have been over a dozen internationally comparable tests of student knowledge in mathematics and science, and each points to large differences between the skills of our students and those of many other countries' students. As figure 1 shows, according to the most recent PISA tests of 15-year-olds, we are competing with Latvia, Hungary, and Portugal—and just slightly ahead of Spain and Italy. (PISA is the Programme for International Student Assessment, a set of tests administered every three years across approximately seventy countries.) These are not the countries to which we want to be compared.

Canada, however, does much better than the United States. Canada is culturally and economically comparable to the United States, so it is worth noting that its students do significantly better than ours. The figure also highlights performance in Germany and Finland, countries that provide other possible benchmarks for US performance and to which we refer when considering the economic implications of school improvement.

WHY IT IS IMPORTANT

Differences in performance on these tests are reliable indicators of skills that are important economically. In today's knowledge-based economy, skills drive future productivity gains and economic growth. And it is growth that determines the economic well-being of the country.

The importance of cognitive skills can be seen in figure 2, which plots average annual growth rates in real per capita GDP over the period 1960–2000 for fifty countries (all that have data on economic growth and test scores). This figure provides "conditional" growth and test scores because underlying it is a statistical analysis that also accounts for differences in income in 1960, since it is easier to grow fast if all you have to do is copy what other countries are doing.[1]

Figure 1. **International Mathematics and Science Performance**

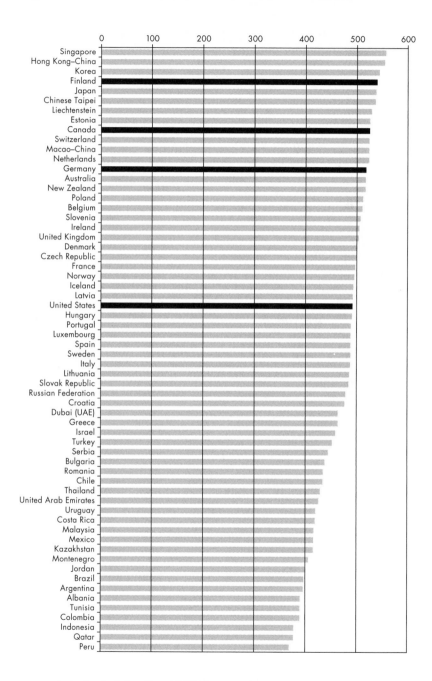

SOURCE Author's calculations from OECD (2010, 2013).

Figure 2. **Economic Growth and Achievement
in Mathematics and Science, 1960–2000**

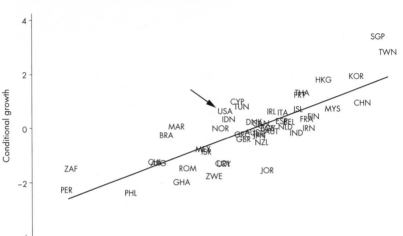

NOTE This added variable plot is derived from a regression of average annual growth
in GDP per capita on test scores, GDP per capita in 1960, and average years of school
attained in 1960; see Hanushek and Woessmann (2015), Table 3.1.
SOURCE Hanushek and Woessmann (2015).

As can be seen, a large portion of the variations in growth rates
can be explained by the test score performance across nations.
The statistical analysis behind this graph also supports a causal interpretation of this relationship. In other words, if a nation finds
a way to improve the skills of its youth measured by these tests, it
can reasonably expect its long-run growth rate to improve.

The United States falls in the middle of the distribution. Moreover, because of historic advantages—having good economic institutions that support growth, historically strong investments in
human capital, the best colleges and universities, and a supply
of strong immigrants—the US performance was better than expected (i.e., it is above the line).

These differences in growth portrayed in the figure are very important. We can use the historic impact of skills on growth to project the economic implications of improving our schools. It turns out that this is a very steep line and improvements in skills (as measured by these international tests) would have a dramatic impact on the future of the United States. Moving from the current US position to the top of the test score distribution would, by the historical relationship, raise growth by 2 percentage points. US per capita GDP growth has been less than 2 percent lately, so this would more than double our growth rate.

Moving to the top of world achievement rankings is clearly very difficult, but more realistic improvements yield enormous gains. Table 1 provides estimates of the economic value of improving achievement by varying amounts. The achievement targets are those of Germany, Canada, and Finland, and the table shows projections of the economic gains that could be expected from having US students reach these levels over a twenty-year period. The economic gains simply assume that the historical growth relationship depicted in figure 2 holds into the future and that the quality of the labor force progressively improves as new, better-educated workers replace retiring ones. The impacts on growth are projected over an eighty-year period (the life expectancy of somebody born today). The economic gains are the difference in GDP expected with no improvement in schools versus the improvement to Germany, Canada, or Finland, and all future values are discounted so that we can calculate the present value of these gains. (The present value is simply how much future gains in income are worth today, and this allows the overall gains for future periods to be directly compared to values of GDP today.)

From table 1, bringing our schools up to the level of Germany over a two-decade period would yield a present value of $43.8 trillion, an enormous value compared to our current GDP of about $17 trillion. The present value is 2.58 times current GDP, or an increase in the level of GDP by more than 6 percent of what is expected with no change in schools.[2] This average increase in

Table 1. **Economic Value of Alternative Improvements in US Achievement**

	Being Germany	Being Canada	Being Finland	Achieving NCLB
Present value (trillion $)	$43.8	$82.2	$111.9	$86.2
Present value (as a % of current GDP)	258%	482%	658%	507%
Average % increase in future GDP level	6.2%	11.4%	15.8%	12.1%

SOURCE Eric A. Hanushek, Paul E. Peterson, and Ludger Woessmann, *Endangering Prosperity: A Global View of the American School* (Washington, DC: Brookings Institution Press, 2013).

GDP more than covers all projected federal deficits, solves the Social Security and Medicare funding problems, and leaves added money for many other purposes.

The gains for reaching the schooling level of Canada or Finland go up from there. Attaining Canadian levels would lift the level of GDP by more than 11 percent. This increase is roughly equivalent to an average increase of paychecks for all workers of over 20 percent. Reaching Finnish levels is worth over $100 trillion in present value.

The final column in table 1 considers the impact of reaching the goal of No Child Left Behind (NCLB) of having all children at proficiency levels (except this would not occur for another twenty years, instead of 2014, as envisioned in the original legislation). Reaching NCLB would, by historical patterns, raise the level of GDP by 12 percent.

What students learn in school matters far more than how long they go to school. Statistical analysis of differences in growth across countries indicates that differences in the number of years of schooling have no separate impact on economic growth once cognitive skills, or learning, are taken into account. Early cognitive development leads people to get more schooling, and early K-12 learning strongly influences the skills they will acquire with later schooling and college. Emphasizing attainment (such as high school graduation) without considering the quality of learning does not make sense.

SOURCES OF IMPROVEMENT

Improving schools, while the professed goal of the public and of politicians since Sputnik, has proven difficult. Spending on schools has dramatically increased, showing a quadrupling in real terms since 1960. Yet the performance since 1970 of seventeen-year-olds has been constant in mathematics and reading (according to the National Assessment of Educational Progress, or NAEP).

The increases in spending have gone largely toward dramatic declines in pupil-teacher ratios (from 25.8:1 in 1960 to 15.3:1 in 2008). Real teacher salaries have also gone up, but more modestly: an 8 percent increase from 1994 to 2008. Unfortunately, research shows that these are not the things that drive improvements in student outcomes.

The most consistent factor affecting student achievement is the quality of teachers. The differences in teacher quality are startling.

A direct way of seeing the potential impact of teachers is to look at differences in the growth of student achievement across teachers. It is natural to define good teachers as those who consistently obtain high learning growth from students, while poor teachers are those who consistently produce low learning growth. A substantial number of studies of learning gains (or value-added) of teachers exist, and they indicate clearly how much difference can come to a student based on teacher assignment. In one study, teachers near the top of the quality distribution got an entire year's worth of additional learning out of their students compared to teachers near the bottom. Importantly, this analysis considered kids just from minority and poor inner-city families, indicating that family background is not fate and that good teachers can overcome deficits that might come from poorer learning conditions in the home.

A second perspective comes from combining existing quantitative estimates of differences in teacher quality with achievement gaps by race or income. Having a good teacher as opposed to an average one for three to four years in a row would, by available estimates, close the average achievement gap by income. Closing the black-white achievement gap, which is a little larger than the average income gap, would take good teachers three and a half to five years in a row.

But, perhaps the most salient perspective for the discussion of teacher salaries is to calculate the impact of effective teachers on the future earnings of students. A teacher who raises the achievement of a student will tend, other things being equal, to raise earnings throughout that student's work life. Using 2010 earnings, for example, a teacher in the seventy-fifth percentile (when compared to the average teacher) would on average raise each student's lifetime income by somewhat more than $14,300. With a class of twenty-five students, this teacher would add $358,000 in future income compared to an average teacher.[3]

Figure 3 shows the total contribution of teachers at the sixtieth, seventy-fifth, and ninetieth percentile compared to an average teacher and how this varies with the number of students taught. Excellent teachers add over $800,000 to the students in a class of thirty. Even a teacher just above average at the sixtieth percentile would add over $100,000 to a class of twenty students. These are calculations for each school year. These above-average teachers add hundreds of thousands of dollars to their students' lifetime earnings.

But there is also the darker side. Below-average teachers subtract from student earnings at a similar rate. The tenth percentile teacher, compared to an average teacher, subtracts over a half-million dollars per year for each group of twenty students he teaches. For the tenth, twenty-fifth, and fortieth percentile

Figure 3. **Impact on Student Lifetime Incomes by Class Size
and Teacher Effectiveness (compared to average teacher)**

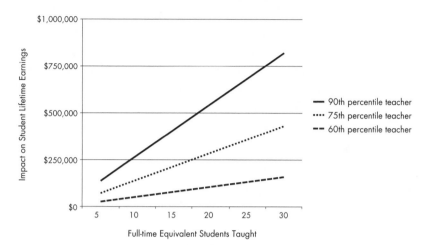

SOURCE Hanushek, Eric A. 2011. "The Economic Value of Higher Teacher Quality,"
Economics of Education Review 30, No. 3 (June): 466–479.

teacher, one simply has to put a minus sign in front of the values
seen in figure 3.

Summarizing decades of research on education, we find that
high-quality teachers are the most important ingredients in education. Regardless of class size, facilities, tests, standards, and
curriculum, no factor makes a greater difference to education
outcomes than better teachers.[4]

INSTITUTIONAL STRUCTURES AND
INCENTIVES IN THE SCHOOL SYSTEM

Existing evidence suggests some clear general policies, each of
which is related to incentives that ensure hiring and retaining
high-quality teachers and administrators. The relevant incentives,
in turn, are created by the institutions of the education system—
the rules and regulations that set rewards and penalties for the
people involved in the education process.

From existing research, four interrelated policies come to the forefront. School systems must: evaluate and reward directly good teacher performance; promote more competition, so that parental demand will create strong incentives to improve individual schools; offer greater autonomy in local decision-making, so that individual schools and their leaders can take actions to promote student achievement; and set up an accountability system that demands good school performance and rewards results.

Direct rewards. Given the importance of high teacher quality, a candidate for improvement is the specific form of accountability that aims incentives directly at teachers. While convincing evidence on the effects of performance-related teacher pay is scarce, the more rigorous studies in terms of empirical identification tend to find a positive relationship between financial incentives for teachers and student outcomes.

Most existing evaluations of performance pay systems nonetheless focus on whether existing teachers change their behavior—what is referred to as the "effort" margin. There are many reasons to believe, however, that the "selection" margin—the attraction of new teachers and the retention of the more effective ones—is more important. The importance of pay for selection is difficult to analyze because it generally involves considering longer-run incentives and the evaluations must focus on moves of teachers in and out of schools. One evaluation keyed to the selection margin in schools in Washington, DC, where the pay and retention system emphasizes rewarding the best teachers while dismissing the worst, finds strong achievement results.[5] Cross-country variation provides some indication that students perform better in countries that allow for teacher salaries to be adjusted based on performance in teaching. For example, the introduction of performance-related pay had a substantial positive impact on student achievement in England. From a comparison across countries, there is evidence that aggregate changes in salaries over time lead to higher student performance. At the school level, monetary incentives for teachers based on their students' performance have also been shown to improve student learning very significantly in Israel and in India.[6]

A key element of rewarding performance is having a good evaluation system that can fit into the personnel system. On this score, a majority of states have made gains, largely in terms of linking a portion of evaluations to the performance of students. These changes have occurred through the actions of state legislatures, although the courts have also been involved.[7] An important California court case (*Vergara v. California*) ruled that a set of state tenure and dismissal laws were unconstitutional because they harmed the children who must be in classes with teachers who otherwise would have been dismissed.[8]

In sum: by far the most effective way to get good teachers is for schools to be able to fire teachers who do poorly, to make way for more promising candidates. It does no good to attract good teachers with higher salaries if there are no slots for them to work, or if they are the first to be fired under age- or tenure-based contracts. The "selection" margin is far more effective in teaching than the "effort" margin, as it is in every other business. And this margin is effectively closed in most of America's public schools.

School accountability. It is difficult to imagine any reform programs—whether those of autonomy, choice, direct performance rewards, or others—working well without a good system of student testing, measurement, and accountability. Thus, the ideas about the various institutional structures are closely linked, since an accountability system provides for linking other incentives to student outcomes.

Many countries around the world have been moving toward increased accountability of local schools for student performance. The United Kingdom has developed an elaborate system of "league tables" designed to give parents full information about the performance of local schools. The United States had a federal law (No Child Left Behind) that all states must have an accountability system that meets certain general guidelines, although this was replaced in 2015 by a new federal system (Every Student Succeeds Act). Under this new law, individual states have considerably increased latitude in designing their accountability system; the results of this change are currently unknown.

Evidence on the impact of accountability systems has begun to accumulate. While there is some uncertainty, the best US evidence indicates that strong state accountability systems lead, in fact, to better student performance.[9]

Combining accountability with parental choice are systems that give students in schools that repeatedly do badly on the accountability test a voucher to attend private schools. In Florida, the threat of becoming subject to private-school choice has been shown to increase teacher and school performance, particularly to the benefit of disadvantaged students.[10] Unfortunately, the Florida courts ruled that this approach violated the state constitution. Courts and constitutions in other states likely would not come to the same conclusion.

Curriculum-based external exit exams are another means to introduce some form of accountability into the school system. Students in countries with external-exit exam systems tend to systematically outperform students in countries without such systems. In Canada and Germany, the two federal education systems where the existence of external exams varies across regions, students similarly perform better in regions with external exams.[11]

Choice or autonomy will not work well without a good system of student testing and accountability. Thus, the ideas about institutional structure are closely linked. The international evidence, as described below, clearly suggests that school autonomy—in particular local autonomy over teacher salaries and course content—is only effective in school systems that have external exams. For example, school autonomy over teacher salaries is negatively associated with student achievement in systems without external exams, but positively in external-exam systems. These findings reflect simple economic logic: with autonomy in decisions, local schools might pursue other interests than just raising student achievement unless performance is public knowledge and unless that performance is measured in a consistent way across schools.

Choice and competition. Choice and competition through school vouchers were proposed a half-century ago by Milton Friedman. The simple idea is that parents, interested in the schooling outcomes of their children, would seek out productive schools, yielding demand-side pressure that creates incentives for each school to produce effective education and ensure high-quality staff in addition to a good curriculum. Schools that fail to do this could be forced to shut down, and new schools that do better could open, expand, and thrive.

In many school systems around the world (with the Netherlands being the most obvious example), privately managed schools (with public funding) provide alternatives for students. In the United States, there are limited examples of private school choice, ranging from publicly funded school vouchers in Milwaukee, Cleveland, and Washington, DC, to privately financed voucher alternatives. The evaluations of these generally show that the choice schools do at least as well as the regular public schools, if not better.

Autonomy and decentralization. Several institutional features of a school system can be grouped under the heading of autonomy or decentralization, including fiscal decentralization, local decision-making on different matters, and parental involvement. Almost any system of improved incentives for schools depends upon having school personnel in individual schools and districts heavily involved in decision-making. There is no point to incentives if people cannot respond to them. It is difficult to compile evidence on the impact of autonomy, because the degree of local decision-making is a decision for a country (or state) as a whole, leaving no comparison group within countries.

American states have varying amounts of local autonomy. One

systematic form of school autonomy is charter schools—public schools that are allowed to perform quite autonomously. (Note that these are actually hybrids of choice schools and public-school autonomy, because they survive only if sufficient numbers of students attend them.) The evidence on them is mixed, but indicates a variety of places where charter schools outperform the regular public schools after the initial start-up phase. But it also suggests in part that the regulations governing them and the particular competitive public schools they face have an influence. For example, charters in Massachusetts perform much better relative to traditional public schools while the opposite is true for charters in Indiana or Illinois, but the precise causes are unknown.[12]

Summary of Incentive Policies. One of the overarching conclusions from the evidence on incentive programs is that the policies tried so far contain no miracles that will dramatically improve the public schools. Each of the policies above has general support from the evidence; but the evidence suggests that each alone, as implemented so far, is incapable of erasing our educational problems. While some suggest that the existing changes—charters or accountability, for example—are radical reforms that may have gone too far, the evidence suggests the opposite. Not only do we have to push harder on the incentives that we know have positive impacts but also we have to actively consider truly dramatic options. As we have seen, the costs of not improving our schools are extraordinarily large, and they warrant equally as large changes in parental choice, teacher evaluations and pay, and strengthened accountability.

OTHER EDUCATION PROGRAMS AND POLICIES

The problems of K-12 performance are the most severe educational problems facing the United States. There are, however, a number of other commonly discussed issues that deserve mention. These include early childhood education, the cost of higher education, and Common Core. No attempt is made to describe these issues completely. The objective is simply to point out some of the larger concerns.

Early Childhood Education. Considerable recent attention has gone to discussing the importance and availability of early childhood education. There are two primary parts to this discussion. First, research shows that early education is particularly valuable because subsequent learning builds on it. Second, disadvantaged children are less likely to have high-quality early childhood education than more advantaged children. Both parts are backed by evidence.

These facts, however, do not indicate the correct policies that might be pursued. In particular, the gains for early childhood programs are concentrated in poor families. Providing fully subsidized programs to all participants would be a significant transfer to middle- and upper-income families. Additionally, little is known about the elements of a high-quality program that might be more broadly run. The strongest evidence about program effectiveness (from the Perry Preschool and Abecedarian projects) comes from very expensive programs that exceed anything that might become a widespread governmental program. Effective policymaking in this area simply requires more information.

The federal government currently runs a very large early childhood program: Head Start. When evaluated, however, it has never been shown to be a very efficacious program. The most recent evaluation suggests no lasting effects from the program. Thus, a component of improved early childhood education would be a redesign of the Head Start program, including its possible complete elimination and replacement.

Higher Education. US colleges and universities are generally regarded as the best in the world, and they consistently attract top students from other countries. Two issues have received widespread publicity and discussion: access and cost.

The economic returns to completing college are very large and have grown in recent decades in many (but not all) subject degrees. In large part, these returns reflect the development of new technologies that are more and more skill-dependent. Thus, if many people do not have ready access to college, that will have downstream implications for incomes and economic well-being.

The biggest concern about access to higher education revolves around the preparation of students for more advanced material—precisely the point of the discussions about the state of K-12 education. The largest barrier to attending and completing higher education is the lack of an earlier development of the requisite skills.

The expense side of higher education has received the most attention recently, focusing on rising tuitions and the size of loan debts. This discussion must, however, be put into perspective. The most rapid rise in tuition and fees has occurred among public two- and four-year institutions (which comprise 72 percent of the market). In real terms, between 2000 and 2012 there was a 63 percent increase in tuition and fees in public institutions (compared to a 37 percent increase in private, not-for-profit institutions).

Two observations should be made. First, at the average 2012 tuition of $5,500 ($7,700 in public four-year colleges), there is still a very large positive return to college for most students. It would, of course, be a larger return if the tuition were smaller, but the economic future for the typical college graduate far exceeds that of a non-completer. Second, the tuition at public institutions is only part of the cost, with the state taxpayers contributing the remaining portion. The rise in tuition reflects a changing source of funding, moving away from general taxpayers toward student-recipients of valuable higher education. Pushing states to hold down tuition means that the general taxpayers—including all those who did not receive the benefits of subsidized college education—pay a larger share and that the student-recipients get even larger subsidies. This does not seem to be good policy.

Common Core. The recent controversy over the introduction of the Common Core standards has absorbed much of the national debate on education policy. Its proponents argue that it is important to lift the quality of education in the United States to emphasize higher-order thinking and to deliver college- and career-ready students. Further, because the US population is closely linked across states, it does not make sense to have students educated to different levels. Opponents argue that the Common Core was heavily pushed by the federal government—which should not be involved in the curriculum, legally a state function. Additionally, the Common Core standards in a number of instances seem less rigorous than those already in place in some states.

While there is considerable appeal to the idea of having high nationwide standards, there is a substantial difference between declaring what students should know and having them actually know what is in the standards. Because the debate around the existence of Common Core has become so expansive, basic policy issues have been neglected—and it is these issues that are more important in improving the learning of our students. In fact, because of the change in testing that has accompanied adoption of the Common Core, a number of states have suspended their accountability systems for teachers and schools.

On each of these policy issues—preschool, higher education, and Common Core—there has been substantial public discussion; but much of it has not been very productive in terms of improving the overall performance of the US education system. The issues may have political appeal, but political appeal does not form the basis of strong policy development.

FEDERAL ROLE

The appropriate role for the federal government warrants separate consideration. Public education in the United States is a state function, with the states also delegating much authority to local school districts. The federal government had little involvement in K-12 education until the Elementary and Secondary Education Act of 1965, when Washington pointed to education as an important part of the War on Poverty.

The primary federal government involvement in K-12 education has focused on disadvantaged and special education students. For higher education, the federal government has emphasized aid in the form of loans and grants to students.

The federal government currently provides about 10 percent of the funding for K-12 education. It also has been heavily involved in school accountability through NCLB, which was developed in the 2001 re-authorization of the Elementary and Secondary Education Act, although that has recently changed.

What should the education role of federal government be? While the answer to this question can be somewhat controversial (as seen in the Common Core debates), it seems necessary for the federal government to pursue a few central roles.

First, Washington must take a national leadership role in promoting the importance of world-class education for the United States. This includes a bully pulpit to specify and promote what we need to achieve with our schools. It is perfectly legitimate for the federal government to help to define the goals of schools, and even the measurement of these through testing. The Common Core dispute is largely that the federal government overstepped its role by putting undue pressure on the states to adopt the federal model.

Second, the federal government should continue supporting disadvantaged and special education students. These populations are important not only from an equity/fairness perspective but also to fully develop our human capital. At the same time, these are populations that need extra resources, and the federal government should ensure their support regardless of where the populations are located. To date, the federal government has focused on mandating state actions, but it might take a page from the Florida approach of providing vouchers directly to special education students.

Third, continued support for low-income students in colleges and universities through grants and loans is by the same logic a natural role for the federal government.

Fourth, Washington should tackle the lack of reliable evidence about programs and policies that is needed to inform education policymaking. The federal government is the natural place to locate research and evaluation activities, because states and districts across the country can all benefit from sound research on general problems. Individual states will tend to underinvest in research activities because they do not directly see the value of this research to other states. And given the size and importance of the education sector, the current amount of support for research is woefully low.

Fifth, the federal government should ensure that high-quality data are available to qualified researchers pursuing the continued expansion of policy-relevant knowledge. The quality and importance of research in education has, without question, grown, particularly spurred by the data on student outcomes that has come from administrative records. Two related issues are testing ("opting-out") and conditions for accessing student records. Widespread opting-out of testing has the effect of destroying the usefulness of testing data for accountability and for evaluations that can improve programs.

There are also roles that are inappropriate for the federal government. NCLB highlighted this fact. The structure of NCLB essentially had the states decide what was to be accomplished by schools while the federal government specified how education should take place if schools did not produce satisfactory results. These roles are the opposite of what they should be. The federal government is in the best position to specify what needs to be produced, but it is quite unprepared to direct what 100,000 schools should do to accomplish this. The states should be given the "how" role. The Every Student Succeeds Act gives more latitude to the states, but it is yet to be seen whether the general principles of accountability for results remain solidly in play.

CONCLUSIONS

The future of the United States is dependent on the skills of its population. A basic problem is that improving these skills, which depends on enhancing the quality of schools, takes a long and consistent policy regime. This has to come from leadership at the top.

The states have primary responsibility for the schools, but the federal government can and should be an important actor in setting the agenda and ensuring that the agenda is accomplished.

CHAPTER 9

TRADE AND IMMIGRATION

John H. Cochrane

Six months of xenophobic political bloviation do not overturn centuries of experience. Trade and immigration are good for the US economy.

As Adam Smith and David Ricardo explained two centuries ago, it is better for England to make wool and Portugal to make wine, and to trade, than for each country to do both. English wine-makers likely disagreed.

The founders understood the benefits of immigration, complaining in the Declaration of Independence that King George ". . . has endeavored to prevent the population of these States; for that purpose obstructing the Laws for Naturalization of Foreigners; refusing to pass others to encourage their migrations hither."

Their Constitution brilliantly forbids internal protectionism against the movement of goods and people, setting up the world's largest free trade and free migration zone and, not coincidentally, what became the wealthiest nation on Earth.

Two centuries of economic scholarship have only deepened and reinforced these lessons. We now recognize that much trade occurs among similar countries: the United States and Canada, not England and Portugal. This fact tells us that specialization of production and knowledge, the dizzying variety of goods a modern economy produces, and increasing returns are deeper sources of trade patterns than simple facts like British vs. Portuguese weather. But the fact that your car—even an "American" one—is produced from parts made in a hundred different countries remains vital to the low cost and high quality of the car you buy today.

Much trade also now travels on wires, not on boats, in the form of specialized services. Yet trading the best and most efficiently provided services from around the world—Hollywood movies and Silicon Valley software for Indian call centers and radiology readings, for example—is just as important to our economy as trading wine for wool.

Trade is already pretty free. The challenge is mostly to preserve and extend what we have and to avoid one of those periodic global disasters such as the 1930s, when the world slid into trade barriers, or occasional national disasters of isolationism, protectionism, and *Juche* (North Korean for self-reliance).

Immigration is largely not free, so many of its potential benefits remain unrealized. Michael Clemens, reviewing current scholarship in the *Journal of Economic Perspectives*, summarizes current knowledge with the ballpark estimate that reducing barriers to immigration could *double* world income per capita.

In the last few decades, economists have also come to a much better understanding of the sources of long-run growth. This understanding only reinforces the importance of trade and openness. Economic growth itself depends on globalization, expanding the number of people with whom we trade ideas, skills, and goods. If you live in a village of one hundred, or even a small country of ten million, inventing an iPhone makes no sense. You'll never sell enough to recoup the costs. It only makes sense to innovate if you can sell it in a global market of billions of people. Growth comes from ideas, ideas are hard to come by, and expertise is specialized. The more people you are connected with, the more you grow. "The division of labor is limited by the extent of the market," noted Adam Smith, and 250 years of work have fleshed out just how deep that observation is.

Against this backdrop, the economic and political discussion

surrounding trade and migration remains stubbornly protectionist, mercantilist, and xenophobic.

In response to such forces, invoking study after study will do
as much good as invoking a thousand scientific articles supporting Darwin at a revival meeting. The most good one can do is to
point out the many simple logical fallacies adduced in the cause
of restricting people's rights to buy and sell what they want, to
hire whom they want, and to move, produce, and live where they
want. You're being sold a bill of goods by people who want to use
the power of the government to pick your pocket. At least recognize the snake oil.

It is perhaps understandable that the average person falls for
economic fallacies. Individual experience as a worker or business-
person is a poor guide to the workings of an economy. We call
this the *fallacy of composition* in economics. Each of us individually can get ahead if the government will force our neighbors to
buy from us. But the country as a whole cannot get ahead by this
means—though, heaven knows, our government tries.

But these traps are not an excuse for political leaders to ignore
hundreds of years of solid knowledge and experience. The laws
of physics are counterintuitive, too. Everyday experience suggests
that the earth is flat. Advocating flat-earth public policy in search
of votes is not excusable.

JOBS, JOBS, JOBS

The major objections to free trade and more open immigration
are that they will cost American jobs. To a lesser extent, trade is
also about defending the profits of American exporting companies, which happily fund lobbying for protectionism. But they
defend their actions in the name of jobs.

The logic that isolation will create more American jobs is false.
But it is so pervasive, we must dissect its fallacies.

Follow the money. When a Chinese company sells a product in
America, we send money to China. The Chinese do not sit on the

money. They use a lot of the money to quickly turn around and buy American goods. To the extent that they do not, they use the money to buy things from other countries—iron ore from Australia, oil from the Middle East, food, and an increasing amount of low-wage manufactured items and parts for its own manufacturing. The recipients of these dollars then turn around and spend them on goods from the United States.

To the extent that all the dollars don't end up buying American goods, foreigners end up buying assets in America, investing in our businesses. To the extent they do not buy private assets, they invest in our government bonds, financing deficits and US government spending that would otherwise vanish.

Every dollar comes back. This isn't theory. It isn't an "on the other hand" proposition. It's simple arithmetic. And it doesn't just come out even. Since, pretty much by definition, the foreign goods we buy are better or cheaper, and our goods better or cheaper there, each country is better off.

As often in economics, the problem is that of the seen and unseen. We see and hear from the worker who loses his job due to competition from abroad or to a new immigrant. We do not hear from and see the new job or business created by the foreign worker's expenditure or the low-cost product enhancing the lives of widely dispersed American consumers. The politician can campaign on the doorstep of the "saved" factory. But it's hard for him or her to take credit for nebulous increases in demand and employment spread throughout the economy or the appearance of an even cheaper jar of pickles at Wal-Mart.

When you follow the money, it becomes clear that even foreign tax benefits and subsidies for their industries cannot make America worse off, as a whole. Sure, the industry in the United States that must compete with a subsidized foreigner does worse. But the subsidized foreigner sells to us in exchange for money, and the money must come back. The foreign subsidy ends up distorting American output, but does not lower output or jobs overall.

If the foreign country subsidizes all of its industries, the exchange rate must rise, undoing the subsidy.

Arguments against trade and immigration apply domestically too. If it is wise for the United States to protect a job or business in New York from a cheaper competitor in Beijing, an immigrant from Poland, or a machine made in the United Kingdom, why is it not wise for the state of New York to protect that same job or business from a cheaper competitor in South Carolina, an immigrant from Louisiana, or a machine made in Santa Clara, California? The person losing the job or the lost business doesn't care where the competitors come from.

Most Americans understand that free movement of people and goods between states benefits all of the states' economies and sniff the fallacy of local protectionism. Economics does not know national boundaries, so there is no argument for international protection that would not apply to national protection also.

The process of economic growth *is* painful. New, more efficient businesses come in and displace old, less efficient ones. In a competitive economy, anyone earning rents—extra compensation and an easy life—is a target for growth-producing disruption. Southwest and JetBlue disrupted United, TWA, and Pan Am (remember them?) and their employee unions. A&P put mom and pop out of business, Wal-Mart destroyed A&P, and Amazon.com may displace Wal-Mart. Uber is upending the taxi businesses. And we're all getting cheaper and better goods and services as a result. Lots of people are doing well working for the new businesses. You might argue against "better" in the case of air travel. But that's your choice: 1970 air travel at 1970 prices is still available. It's called "business class." The free market gives you better choices.

People who lose jobs or businesses to foreign competition *are* hurt—just as people who lose jobs and businesses to domestic competition and innovation are hurt. But as I hope these examples emphasize, the churn due to foreign competition is a lot lower than the churn due to domestic competition. It just comes from foreigners, who are easier to demonize.

The lump-of-labor fallacy. Adam Davidson, writing in the *New York Times*, explains a central misconception: "The chief logical mistake we make is something called the Lump of Labor Fallacy: the erroneous notion that there is only so much work to be done and that no one can get a job without taking one from someone else. . . . This argument is wrong."

The lump-of-labor fallacy pervades thinking about trade and immigration, as well as many other misguided laws and policies. In the popular imagination, there are only so many jobs to be had. There are more people who want to work than there are jobs. Unemployment consists of people waiting around for a job to be "created," especially by a politician hungry for a moment on camera.

This vision has nothing to do with reality. In the end, the number of jobs in the United States is the number of people scaled by the fraction who want to work. China has 764 million jobs, while America has 159 million. China didn't take 700 million jobs from the United States—we don't have that many people. China simply has a much larger population.

Jobs is a nonsense argument. Economists who defend or attack trade on the basis of "jobs" are pandering to fallacious political rhetoric.

It is more reasonable to worry that trade and immigration affect wages, not numbers employed. But follow the money again. If by protecting an industry, the government can raise wages or profits in that industry, the money must come from somewhere. Where? Higher prices paid by consumers. When the government deliberately hobbles the productivity of the American economy, by skewing employment to less productive industries, we can only lower wages overall.

We can see direct evidence against the lump-of-labor fallacy in our own history. One of the greatest job invasions in all US history was the increase in women working. Women's labor force participation rose from 32 percent to 60 percent from 1950 to 2000. But 27 percent of men are not permanently out of work now as a result. In the "great migration," about six million African Americans moved from the rural South to Northern cities. Despite widespread fears, riots, and shameful efforts to exclude these newcomers, six million whites did not suffer permanent unemployment as a result.

There has also been huge resistance to national free trade—mills moving from New England to the South, car companies relocating from Detroit to Indiana and Tennessee. Our state and local governments compete to waste taxpayer money on special deals for large employers. That political resistance doesn't make the economics any more logical.

The great churn. The great churn of the US labor force most clearly belies the lump-of-labor fallacy, together with trade protectionism, anti-immigrant protectionism, and all sorts of political efforts to subsidize specific industries in the name of "jobs."

In the single month of January 2016, 4.9 million people in the United States lost their jobs, out of a labor force of 159 million. At that rate, 60 million people, 40 percent of the labor force, will be out of a job by the end of the year. Why is this not a catastrophe? Because in the same month, five million people in the United States got new jobs. The 100,000 new jobs "created" in that month, and bandied in the press, are not a 100,000 expansion in the lump of labor; they are the net difference of a great churn.

For this reason, net employment in the United States is essentially unaffected by protection. If a political intervention could create 100,000 new jobs (if!), that is a drop in the bucket of an economy that creates five million new jobs a month.

The utter incoherence of trade and immigration policy is a good sign of its dysfunction. Trade and immigration policy is mostly about labor protection. Republicans are against immigration, and are turning against trade, all under the banner of protecting American jobs. But why are they then against unions, minimum wages, the Equal Employment Opportunity Commission and the National Labor Relations Board, occupational licensing, and all the rest of the government's misguided job- and business-protection efforts? Democrats are for all those labor protections, but then soft on immigration. The inevitable conclusion: most policy discussion favoring trade and immigration restrictions has other objectives.

IMMIGRATION

The charge that immigrants compete for jobs and drive down American wages needs special attention. Again, this competition is not demonstrably much of a problem. Study after study has found very small impacts of immigrants on American wages.

There are good reasons for this finding. Immigrants come to take jobs Americans don't want. Immigrant labor often complements American labor, allowing the American workers higher pay. If labor does not or cannot move in, capital moves out.

Most of all, *immigrants are demanders, too.* (Another case of "follow the money.") Immigrants work and occupy jobs, yes. But they spend money, too! Every immigrant wants a car, a house, a haircut, food, clothes, and so on. The number of jobs in the United States expands to fill these demands.

If immigrants steal jobs, ask yourself how 159 million Americans have jobs now. We are immigrants or descendants of immigrants. The answer is, we created new businesses and new demand just as much as we created new workers. So will the new immigrants.

Immigration policy is particularly nonsensical. We do not need to go to the extreme of open borders to make enormous strides (although it's worth asking just why not). America would benefit a great deal from small and sensible immigration reform.

Restrictions on high-skilled immigrants, especially kicking out people who complete advanced degrees here, are completely self-destructive. These people want to start businesses, program our computers, innovate, and hire Americans. They share American values better than most native-born Americans. And we kick them out. They would pay taxes, bail out Social Security and Medicare, pay off our government debt, and bail out bankrupt states and localities. And we kick them out.

One might complain about low-skill migrants driving down low-skill American wages, or soaking up more transfers than they receive. I think that this is an unfounded fear. But that complaint makes no sense of our policy of keeping out high-skill, high-wealth, or high-earnings migrants. These will expand the US economy; they will lower inequality by reducing the pressure on high-skilled wages; and they will increase the demand for low-skill workers.

For once, I get to practice what I preach. Higher education has secured itself an exemption from H-1B visa limits. Economics departments and business schools are now largely staffed by foreign-born professors. The result is, by attracting the best minds from around the world, our research universities are centers of excellence and economic innovation. And professorial wages have never been higher.

We could have a very simple policy: if you have $10,000 of assets, a job that pays more than $50,000 (say), and you pay taxes, have health insurance, use no transfers or social services, and have no criminal record, you can work and stay in the United States. We know anyone in this category is contributing to America.

More generally, it is economically nonsensical that our immigration policy is focused on family reunification and (stingily) refugee or political asylum, and denigrates mere economic migrants, while simultaneously complaining of the cost of migrants and their difficulty of assimilating into American life and economy. We should praise and desire economic migrants.

Immigration restrictions based on quantities—a hard cap on

H-1B visas, given out by a lottery that fills in about five minutes— rather than rules and prices is just as nonsensical. A bankrupt government should, at a minimum, charge a price rather than give away valuable goods. More generally, we should set the rules on who we think is a valuable migrant, and let anyone in who follows those rules.

Do we have room for immigrants? America is, in fact, relatively underpopulated. The United States has three and a half million (3,539,225) square miles and eighty-four people per square mile. The United Kingdom has 650 people per square mile. We can let in two billion people and have only the same population density as the United Kingdom. The Netherlands is pretty nice, too, with 1,250 people per square mile, so maybe we have room for four billion.

OK, these are fanciful numbers. But in fact, we are still a lot closer to Jefferson's time than we think, and the United States is in many ways still an underdeveloped country.

Social services and transfers. There is a valid argument that we can't welcome millions of low-income or no-income immigrants overnight and keep up our very progressive tax system, together with the many social programs and benefits we offer low-income people.

That argument, however, makes no sense at all for forbidding high-income immigration. And it makes even less sense for allowing people to come to the United States and then *forbidding* them to work.

Security. Especially in light of recent terrorist attacks, many voices want to restrict immigration to the United States in the name of security. This too is nonsense.

Again, the issue of immigration policy is not who can *enter* the United States. That's the great student and tourist visa debate. (Joke: there is no such debate, of course.) The issue of immigration policy is who is allowed to *work* here.

No terrorist ever swam the Rio Grande and stopped to pick

vegetables for a few years before deciding to blow something up. All our terrorists—and all of Europe's terrorists—are already citizens, home-grown, or here on tourist or student visas . . . and decidedly *not* working.

Europe's problem is assimilation, not immigration, and not hard-working immigrants. Europe's problem is its already too-great protection of its labor markets. When young men cannot break in to protected occupations, when they are forced to lie around in awful neighborhoods, they form an ideal stew for radicalization. Europe's shocking youth unemployment rates are its central problem; promoting assimilation and freeing up its labor markets is the answer.

Europe's policies, allowing many new migrants to enter but then forbidding them to work for years on end, is practically guaranteed to foster a stew of resentments and an expensive and disruptive underclass. It would be better to *require* them to work.

That terrorists might sneak in along with migrants walking from Greece to Germany begs the question: why in 2016 are people *walking* that far anyway? The answer is, that our governments are pretty good at screening people getting on civilized modes of travel such as airplanes. And if they let regular migrants get on airplanes and come to work, a terrorist would have a much harder time sneaking in unnoticed, or he would stand out while walking his way up the Adriatic.

If you still think that immigration restrictions are important for security, ponder this: the border patrol budget is $13 billion. The budget for the *whole FBI* is $6 billion. If you care about security, you want to reverse those numbers.

Social and political values. Some immigration opponents worry that America's social and political values are endangered by immigration, just as their ancestors worried about Irish, German, Italian, Japanese, and Chinese immigrants, to our eternal shame.

Assimilation is an issue. Immigration policy must encourage

it. One can easily demand that immigrants speak English and have a vague understanding of American institutions, history, and law.

If you worry about social values, though, I have bad news for you: you lost that one in the public schools. We barely teach civics any more. Immigrants have to pass a test that most high school students would flunk. And if we welcomed skilled, entrepreneurial immigrants and allowed them to work, we would get the kind who are eternally grateful to be in a country that allows them that freedom.

The consumer and inequality. Arguments about trade and immigration are so often couched in terms of exports, jobs, and wages that we forget the most important objective: the consumer.

The point of trade is for consumers to get better stuff cheaper. A restriction on trade is a restriction on your right, as a consumer and a citizen, to buy the item you want from the best supplier. You are told, instead, that you must buy an inferior item at a higher price from a supplier who has the ear of the federal government, so that your money will subsidize someone else. Restrictions on immigration are restrictions on your right as a consumer or employer to hire the best person for the job; instead, you must hire a worse employee at a higher wage because of the accident of that person's birth.

To the extent that immigrants do reduce American wages, restricting immigration is a horribly inefficient way to subsidize low-skill American labor. Restricting high-skilled immigration or the ability of people to work who are already here and will end up on the public dole otherwise is even more inefficient. If that made sense, it would make sense to forbid half the citizen population from working, to prop up the wages of the other half. The higher wages come from higher prices to the consumer.

Trade and immigration have enormous benefits, especially to lower-income Americans. They can buy cheaper houses, cheaper food, and cheaper cars, and they can shop at Wal-Mart. Manhattan condos and luxury watches are not produced by immigrant labor or abroad.

Allowing more high-skill and high-income immigrants would especially help lower-income Americans. They would spend more and create more jobs. High-skill American wages might decline— but most of the policy world wants that, to reduce inequality due to a lack of high-skilled workers.

POLICY AND RHETORIC

International economists and policy types have hurt their cause by adopting mercantilist rhetoric, and in many cases believing it.

If China sells more to America than America sells to China, that is called a trade "imbalance." Nobody calls the fact that the grocery store sells more food to you than you sell to it an imbalance. Trade always balances: the current and capital accounts always add up to zero.

Efforts to increase productivity are urged as measures to increase "competitiveness." But international trade is not a competition for exports. *International trade is not a competition.* Just as your trade with the grocery store is not a competition. Trade is a cooperation. It's not a zero-sum game.

Trade is not about exports, it's about imports. What do you want a pile of Chinese currency for? Exports are the price you have to pay to get imports. If China really were sending us great stuff below cost, the proper answer would be a polite thank you note, and maybe some flowers.

Furthermore, the overall trade balance has nothing to do with the productivity or "competitiveness" of individual firms. Trade and capital accounts must balance, so unless the country wants to save more abroad, more exports at one firm must be met by more imports or less exports at another, or a change in the exchange rate.

If the United States imports more than it exports, that means foreigners are buying US assets, investing here. There are good reasons they might want to do so—they might be aging faster than us, investment opportunities might be better here than abroad. Yet we call these "imbalances" too, and now "savings gluts."

Policy language is even more Orwellian. Countries are urged by the International Monetary Fund to "restrict capital flows." It sounds like technocratic management of a dam on a river. It is not. It is the act of your government forbidding you from using your hard-earned dollars to buy a foreign car or take a nice vacation.

Trade agreements are really managed mercantilism, not about free trade at all. We will let your politically connected exporters enjoy some rents of our protected markets, and in return you will let some of our politically connected exporters enjoy some rents in your protected markets. Support for free trade need not mean unqualified support for this process.

I looked up the Trans-Pacific Partnership. Media reports count 5,544 pages—three times longer than the King James Bible. Free trade needs one sentence: "American buyers may buy anything they want from anywhere in the world without tariff or quota restriction."

The Overall US Benefits Fact Sheet for the Trans-Pacific Partnership headline reads, "The Trans-Pacific Partnership (TPP) . . . levels the playing field for American workers and American businesses, supporting more Made-in-America exports and higher-paying American jobs. . . . TPP makes sure our farmers, ranchers, manufacturers, and small businesses can compete—and win—in some of the fastest-growing markets in the world. . . . TPP will significantly expand the export of Made-in-America goods and services and support American jobs."

It goes on to describe how TPP will enforce US labor laws and environmental laws on foreign countries; it describes commitments to promote sustainable development and inclusive economic growth, reduce poverty, promote food security, and combat child and forced labor.

"Exports," "jobs," "compete." There is not one word about the consumer's ability to *import* better or cheaper goods or the producer's ability to import better and cheaper parts.

This focus is not necessarily undesirable. If a government's central problem is its temptation to cave in to political pressure from labor and business groups that want government-imposed rents, then a multilateral agreement that limits government's abilities to give rents to its constituencies, in return for other governments' agreements to do the same, represents progress toward freer trade. But if the voter succumbs to a mercantilist mentality—thinking jobs are lumps of labor, trade is a competition for exports, and other countries are hurting us when they send us great stuff cheap—it's hard to blame him or her for that misapprehension. When he or she takes those fallacies to the voting booth, well, which of the 5,544 pages of the TPP, and thousands more of its marketing and press coverage, educated him or her otherwise?

FOREIGN POLICY

Even if the xenophobic bluster on the campaign trail is right, even if trade and immigration do sap American jobs, isolation and protection would only make us wealthier by making other countries poorer. Trade may not be a zero-sum game, but trade restrictions definitely are, or are actually strongly negative-sum. Is that really America's place in the world?

Would we advocate sending the Marines to Mexico to take a poor farmer's cow and goat, to send that wealth to American workers? Would we advocate developing software that could out-hack the Chinese, to find workers there living on $5 a day assembling iPhones, and steal half their salaries, to send it to unionized workers in the United States? I think we would find this prospect revolting. But this is exactly the premise of our zero-sum mercantilists on the left and of our zero-sum isolationists on the right.

If one takes a narrow objective that our government's job is to increase the wealth of American citizens, by any means, even using force to grab it from abroad, then some protection might follow.

But in every other part of our national policy, we broadly value the welfare of people around the globe, and we do not send our armies to impoverish them. We send our armies, at great expense, to defend them. We send our aid to improve their lives (with questionable results, but we try). Restricting trade and immigration puts the harm out of sight, but the harm is there nonetheless.

Many of our charities send cows, goats, and adventuresome high school students anxious to improve their college admissions chances to Do Good in foreign villages. If you really want to improve their standard of living, buying what they have to sell and letting them work in the United States is far more effective.

The vision seems to be that we will impoverish foreign workers by forbidding Americans from buying what they have to sell, thereby forbidding them from acquiring currency to buy from Americans, forbidding them to use their talents when they are much more productive here. But then we will send lots of money to their governments and in government-directed aid projects. That is not a coherent strategy.

Trade and migration dramatically raise global incomes and lower global inequality. The explosion of incomes in China and India—from destitute to mediocre—represents the greatest reduction in global inequality and rise in human welfare since we were all equally poor and miserable before the Industrial Revolution. The economic rise of Japan, South Korea, and other "Asian miracles" came equally on the backs of trade and globalization.

And all of this is good for the United States. Even on narrow self-interest, America is better off in a prosperous growing world than it would be if we were slightly richer in an impoverished world . . . which we would not be, anyway.

Since the beginning of the postwar era, the United States has led the world, quietly and patiently, toward the same kind of trade freedom that we enjoy internally. The benefits have been enormous. We have traditionally been the beacon for migrants and the proof that people can move to a better place and quickly contribute to that country, regardless of their initial language, culture, or politics. To turn our back on those principles now would undo a half-century's worth of patient leadership in a world that seems increasingly on the edge of chaos.

A WORLD AWASH IN CHANGE

George P. Shultz

Reflecting on my time as secretary of state, I worry about the sorry state of the world and my instinct is to say something constructive about the problems. How to start?

Let's begin by reviewing the way to think about foreign and security policy, and how to develop strategy. First, take steps to ensure and show the world that we can achieve what we set out to achieve, that a capacity to execute is always on display. The following example had an impact around the world.

Early in Ronald Reagan's presidency, the US air-traffic controllers struck. People came into the Oval Office and counseled him that this presented very complex problems. He said, "It's not complicated; it's simple. They took an oath of office and they broke it. They're out." All over the world, people thought that Reagan was crazy, but he turned to his secretary of transportation, who had been the chief executive of a large transportation company and who understood the problems and knew how to execute. He kept the planes flying. All over the world, people thought, "This guy plays for keeps. Be careful."

Second, be realistic. Throw away your rose-colored glasses. See the world as it is. That doesn't mean only bad things. Don't be afraid to recognize an opportunity when it comes along.

Portions of this chapter also appear in the book *Learning from Experience* (Hoover Institution Press, 2016).

Third, be strong. Of course, that means military strength; and economic strength is essential to a strong military. But we also need to have self-confidence and strength of purpose in our country.

Fourth, develop a US agenda. What is it that we want to achieve? Be careful not to think initially about the other guy's agenda and adjust to it—or you will be negotiating with yourself.

Then be ready to engage, but be clear: no empty threats. I remember boot camp at the start of World War II. My drill sergeant handed me my rifle and said, "Take good care of this rifle. This is your best friend. And, remember, never point this rifle at anyone unless you are willing to pull the trigger." No empty threats. This boot-camp wisdom, often ignored, is essential wisdom.

THE WORLD TODAY seems almost suddenly awash in change. Economies struggle everywhere, the Middle East is in flames, and national borders seem to mean less than ever before. The proliferation of nuclear weapons and the rising possibility of their use threaten all mankind. There are potentially severe consequences of a warming climate. There is a virtually global effort opposed to the long-standing state system for bringing order to the world. And there are more refugees today than at any time since the end of World War II. All this is in sharp contrast to the economic and security commons that coalesced as the Cold War came to an end.

Let's revisit that formation. After World War II, some gifted people in the Truman administration, along with others, looked back—and what did they see? They saw two world wars; the first was settled in rather vindictive terms that helped lead to the second, in which 50 million people were killed and many others injured and displaced. They saw the Holocaust. They saw the Great Depression and the protectionism and currency manipulation that aggravated it. They said to themselves, *What an abysmal world, and we are part of it whether we like it or not.* They set out to construct something better, and just as they got going, the Cold War emerged. So the Marshall Plan, the Bretton Woods system, NATO, and the doctrine of containment came into being. Gradually, continuing through various administrations and mostly on a nonpartisan basis, a security and economic commons was constructed, with important leadership from the United States, from which everybody benefited.

But that commons is now at risk everywhere, and in many places it no longer really exists. So how did we get here again? And what should we do about it this time?

THE BREAKDOWN OF THE GLOBAL COMMONS

The strategic earthquake now underway began with the turn of the twenty-first century. In the simplest summary, it is an accelerating decline in management of the international state system. Many of the states that constitute the system are struggling with their own problems of governance. At the same time, the system is under deadly attack from enemies outside who are pledged to destroy and replace it.

The state system depends upon respect for the borders of countries, but borders are being softened or have recently been eradicated. Most visible are the actions of Vladimir Putin's Russia. He attacked Georgia in 2008 and wound up carving out two new territorial entities: Abkhazia and South Ossetia. More recently, and partly as a response to the movement of Ukraine in the direction of European rule of law and greater interaction with Western European countries, Putin seized Crimea and is in the process of trying to erase the borders of eastern Ukraine. Russian arms have been fired to shoot down a civilian passenger aircraft. Putin is surely playing a very weak hand, but very aggressively. And now he moves in to the Middle East, no doubt seeking, along with Iran, a dominant position.

Meanwhile, in Western Europe, those in charge are gradually reducing the meaning of borders as they seek to homogenize into

"Europe" all the ancient cultures of that region. The creation of the euro is a case in point. Many economists warned that the coverage of the very different economies in Europe by a fixed exchange rate would lead to trouble: varying degrees of austerity would replace the flexibility of exchange rates, a result that is increasingly unacceptable. The stresses produced by this effort are all too evident as the dispersion of sovereign power leaves a sense of uncertainty and indecisiveness in the region in the face of continuing economic problems.

Of course, the Middle East has become a vivid display of the vast changes in patterns of governance and in the profile of relationships among states. The focus on the Israeli-Palestinian relationship and the US preoccupation with the "peace process" fails to recognize the larger world-historical situation at present. What kind of war is this now being waged in the Middle East and beyond? To better understand, we instead need to revisit the nature of world order as analyzed at the time of the French Revolution. At that time, as is true now, the greatest danger to the international state-based structure comes when an ideology gathers horizontal appeal—when (to borrow Martin Wight's framework) men's loyalties bind them closer to similarly minded men in other states than to their fellow citizens.[1] The consequence, according to Edmund Burke, "is to introduce other interests into all countries than those which arise from their locality and natural circumstances."[2] This was expressed in Marxism-Leninism as "an industrial worker in Marseilles" having "greater solidarity with an industrial worker in Yokohama than either does with the French or Japanese people or nation." And this horizontal ideological solidarity can be turned into a revolution against the established border-defined order of states with mutual obligations and formalized interactions.

This is what underlies the "strategic earthquake" across the Middle East today. The ignition switch that started this new war and turned it into the armed upheaval we saw by the summer of 2014 was a seemingly small incident, but it turned on long-simmering resentment against loss of dignity and the absence of opportunity. In 2011, a lone entrepreneur in Tunisia tried to start a little business selling fruits and vegetables, and the regime squashed him for refusing to pay a bribe. What resonance that act produced! Along with the American overthrow of Iraq's Saddam Hussein and the departures of Hosni Mubarak in Egypt and Zine El Abidine Ben Ali in Tunisia, the lid on full-scale oppression in Iraq and elsewhere was lifted and the idea was aroused of escaping oppression anywhere in the region.

That escape is now conceivable because people know what is going on and can communicate and organize. With the lifting of the lid, out came a seemingly innumerable array of formerly suppressed tribes, factions, sects, ethnicities, causes, and so on that had been building up pressure for generations. Then they began to attack each other out of revenge and for future power-holding. Between 2007 and 2013, it appeared that there were three or four different levels of civil wars going on within the Arab-Muslim world.

This in turn revealed a new reality. The Arab regimes, at least since the post-Second World War period, had been telling the world that all was well in the Middle East except for one thing: the existence of Israel. American administrations across the years generally accepted this narrative and devoted their efforts to a process attempting to resolve the Arab-Israeli conflict. At the same time, the Arab state regimes, starting in the mid-1970s, recognized the growing existence of a horizontal, religiously radical political ideology that held a dangerous potential for the regimes themselves. Some of the regimes, therefore, began to try to co-opt the Islamists by subsidizing them and urging them to redirect their threats away from the regimes and toward Israel and European and American targets.

The overthrow of rulers in Tunisia and Egypt, and of Saddam Hussein's regime, caused the Islamists to envision overthrowing other Arab state regimes. The old narrative was no longer plausible or sustainable; it was now a Muslim-on-Muslim conflict that had nothing to do with Israel. And within this contest was the re-emergence of the centuries-old mutual hatred of Sunnis and Shias. Over the past three or more years, these layers of intra-Muslim conflict have coalesced into one ever-larger civil war between the state regimes that are inside the international state system and the Islamist ideologues who would overthrow the regimes and take the entire region out of the international system and into their religiously driven new world order.

This is what happened in the summer of 2014 with the sudden emergence of the Islamic State of Iraq and al-Sham (ISIS) and its self-proclaimed Islamic State and Caliphate. ISIS's goal was clearly stated by one of its fighters: "We are opposed to countries," that is, to the world of states.

But in addition to the arrival of a territory-holding horizontal military force, another dimension of threat is involved: religion. From the 1648 end of the Thirty Years War, to the mid-1990s, religion was thought to have been neutralized as a cause of conflict in international affairs. Now, religion and religious war have returned. Religion, especially in the premodern period, was largely adversarial to diversity, demanding that all peoples under its purview adhere to a single way of belief and practice. The modern age sought to neutralize this tendency by declaring that while each state could practice the religion(s) of its choice, religious doctrines and scriptures should be kept out of interstate negotiations, a precept that worked well for a long time.

However, after three centuries of keeping religion out of international affairs, the rise of radical Islam in the late twentieth century and on into the twenty-first has been a severe setback to the cause of governing diversity. Radical Islamism finds it intolerable to cooperate with unbelievers, and in recent years there has been an upsurge in such intolerance even within Islam in the Sunni-Shia conflict. So all the factors for a climax are now involved: a horizontal ideology, territorial holdings, religion, and dedication to the destruction of the modern international order.

All this comes at a time when the American grand strategy seems to countries around the world to be one of withdrawal.

WHAT TO DO ABOUT IT?

The authors of the essays which follow weigh in with their own ideas on more strategic approaches to our country's security: across our military forces, our energy picture, and in the craft of diplomacy. Let me start them off by laying out a few key concepts of my own.

As we look at our military, which clearly needs support for its force structure, training, acquisition of weapons, and, even more important, the costly effort to develop weapons of the future, we need to confront the fact of a large and building erosion in the military budget caused by massive health care and pension commitments. Those commitments, if not dealt with, will crowd out the basic functions of the military. They need some of the same medicine as must be applied to entitlements.

Russia is attempting to build and extend a sphere of influence beyond its borders. One of Russia's strengths is the dependence of many countries, particularly in Eastern Europe and the Baltic states, on it for supplies of oil and gas. Russia has demonstrated that it is willing to cut off supplies in the middle of winter, so the first step is to put in place a European energy initiative. The United States has recently developed an ability to produce oil and gas far beyond earlier times, so we should lift the export controls, develop LNG facilities, encourage the use of the new energy production and trade infrastructure in European countries that do have potential capacities, and put in place enough capacity in every country that the threat by Russia to cut off supplies is sharply weakened.

At the same time, we need to see that our military capabilities, working with NATO and urging larger budgets for defense, are strong and present on a proper basis in the countries most threatened. NATO is now developing just these capabilities. And then there is the situation in Ukraine. We need to see that Ukraine's armed forces are trained and equipped. More fundamentally, we need to help Ukraine lessen the corruption in its governmental processes and take advantage of its natural capabilities to get its economy moving in a positive direction.

If we are able to put these policies in place, Russia will see that it is not walking into a vacuum but into a stone wall. Russia is playing such a weak hand—economically and demographically— that we also must be ready to engage with Russia, expecting that at some point along the way Russia will see the advantages of working within a collaborative state system. But in the meantime, Russia has returned to the Middle East in collaboration with Iran, first in support of Bashar Assad's Syrian regime, but, no doubt, in a combined effort to extend Iranian reach as sanctions are lifted.

The Middle East and ISIS present more difficult and complex issues, as we have already outlined. Nevertheless, these imperatives stand out. We must develop the strength to prevail militarily over ISIS. Of course, this means air power; but there must also be boots on the ground that are capable and effective. They will be more effective if they are mostly Arab boots. The challenge is to develop a force in the region that, in coordination with us, can be impactful. An unusual potential coalition is possible: Saudi Arabia, Jordan, Egypt, the United Arab Emirates, and Israel, plus Iraqi Kurds and others with help from traditional European allies.

We also need to do everything we can to limit ISIS's access to financial capability. This means a hard diplomatic effort to persuade Arab states that have a past record of trying to buy off ISIS that such a tactic is self-defeating. Access to oil supplies can be greatly restricted by air power and the denial of access to markets.

With a sharp decline in military success on the part of ISIS, its appeal will decline. Nevertheless, we need to seek ways to understand that appeal and deal effectively with it. Every country in the

West, let alone Russia and China, needs to be on guard against potential terrorist threats that may spring from the ISIS carcass.

An essential ingredient in the development of foreign policy is the maintenance of a constructive relationship with China. Strains are now clearly evident, but they can be dealt with by strong diplomacy. Here's what to do:

The two presidents or, alternatively, their authorized secretaries of state, defense, and treasury should develop a list of all those areas where cooperation and interaction are beneficial to each country. The list will be fairly long, but will be dominated by the economic advantages to both countries of their large economic interaction. There are obvious areas of collaboration in the terrorism, climate, and nuclear arenas. There are also points of tension.

For example, the competing claims with Japan over the Senkaku Islands were quiet for a long while as both sides simply agreed to disagree and put the issue to sleep. Skillful diplomacy should be able to put the issue back to sleep. The South China Sea presents more difficult issues, but perhaps there is a template that could be used. A careful joint study by a council of all the countries with interacting borders, including sea borders, with a rotating chairman can set out and respect the rules. That has been used to deal with issues of the Arctic, so perhaps the Arctic Council can serve as a template.

The problems posed by nuclear weapons are immense and are of vital significance to all countries. The explosion of even a few of these weapons almost anywhere would have disastrous global implications. China and the United States should be partners in taking every possible step to get better control of these weapons of mass destruction. The United States and China could work together with others to create a joint enterprise of countries working on this issue. In May 2016, President Obama hosted a fourth meeting at the heads-of-government level to find ways to get better control of fissile material. Perhaps this meeting could become a launching pad for a global nuclear control enterprise.

At the same time, much progress is being made on the nuclear front in the ability to verify whatever is taking place. Traditional technical means are still available. A template of on-site inspection in the most recent Strategic Arms Reduction Treaty between the United States and Russia is a working arrangement. The Open Skies Treaty still operates reasonably well and the emergence everywhere of information and communication capabilities is making the world more and more an open book. Let's put these possibilities to use in the hope that somehow and some way an end can be put to nuclear weapons. As has been said, "A nuclear war can never be won and must never be fought."

Finally, we must garden. Anyone who tries to grow things knows that if you plant something and then come back six months later, all you will have is weeds. So you learn to keep at it so that you can have a healthy garden.

The same is true in diplomacy. Listen to people, talk to people, and discuss possibilities, problems, and opportunities. Get to know others and build a relationship of trust—even when the particular issues themselves might still be on the back burner. Then, when problems arise, you have a basis for work in a constructive way. Storms may come, but a good gardener will always have good flowers and good crops. I'll have a few more words to say on that in our conclusion, but first let's hear some more on needed outward-facing strategies and international relationships from our Hoover scholars.

CHAPTER 10

RESTORING OUR NATIONAL SECURITY

James O. Ellis Jr., James N. Mattis, and Kori Schake

For the past twenty years, across administrations of both political parties, the United States has been operating largely
unguided by strategy. We have been much too reactive to events
and crises, and have allowed others to define the perception and
outcomes of our engagement around the world.

Since the end of the Cold War, America's strengths have buff-
ered us against many of the consequences of operating without
a strategy, but it is a costly way to do business. It has caused us
to fight wars we could have avoided, and to lose wars we ought
to have won. It has resulted in tactical successes that do not add
up to strategic victories and has cost our country soldiers' and
diplomats' lives, national treasure, and global credibility. We
have been slow to identify emergent threats and unwilling to
prioritize competing interests; we have sent confusing and con-
founding messages to enemies and allies alike and have been incapable of articulating what we stand for—and what we will not
stand for.

As a result, we have squandered opportunities to strengthen
and support an international order manifestly in America's interests, as well as in the interests of all nations that want a peaceful,
prosperous world.

The international system as we know it—and as we created it—is under assault from the forces of entropy that fill vacuums and corrode order when the United States is not actively engaged. These forces include predatory states that prize their own sovereignty but destroy that of others; ideologies that legitimate violence by the disaffected; and liberal societies that have become so upholstered by naïve perceptions of their own safety that they struggle to speak with clarity about their values or act decisively in their interests.

The challenges are substantial, and addressing them will require a significant effort from us. Yet we must not lose sight of the fact that the international order we built from the ashes of World War II is worth defending and strengthening. If we are to arrest the atrophying of America as the guardian of the international order, we must develop a security strategy appropriate for today's world and flexible enough to respond to alternative futures not yet defined.

We must be clear-eyed about the political, social, cultural, historic, ethnic, and religious realities that confront us, without foisting our norms and values onto others. We must be capable of placing our security above the many other things we also value, understanding that in the absence of security all else is moot. We must be willing to work with imperfect allies to stamp out the fires now raging in the Middle East and beyond. We must marry an unsentimental understanding of the real world with fierce resolve to help change things for the better. In short, we must take our own side in the fight because we have a generational responsibility to hand over to our children the same liberties we enjoy. It sounds difficult. It will be difficult. But our predecessors faced even more daunting challenges and prevailed.

The United States continues to have a wide range of means to reassert an order conducive to our security and that of our allies. We have more tools than just threats, military intervention, and economic sanctions. We have the power to intimidate, but we also have the ability to inspire. The beauty of the American order is that most of the world wants us to succeed, and is willing to help us when we are clear about what we are doing, demonstrate that it is in the collective interest, and persevere to attain our goals.

WHEN DIPLOMACY LED TO SUCCESS

Since the end of World War II, America has been preeminent on the international scene, its power so expansive that we have largely been insulated from the consequences of a fraying world order. We have been so strong for so long that we have ignored the truth that losing wars can have real consequences: we shudder at the beheading of one American prisoner, and can scarcely imagine catastrophes of the magnitude of the Bataan death march or an enemy challenge that calls for a supreme national effort to retain our freedoms. We complacently believe there is an inevitable arc of history propelling the success of our humanist ideology, rather than understanding that it has been advanced with strategic decisions and sacrifices by preceding generations.

In this time of post-Cold War primacy, America has tended to rely too heavily on its power of intimidation. When the risks associated with using military force were higher and the tools of financial sanction less well-developed, our country engaged more intensively in setting rules and establishing norms of behavior, creating institutions and getting them to work, fostering cooperation, helping friends solve their problems, expanding the scope of peoples' aspirations, providing development assistance that improves governance, celebrating allies' achievements, and setting friends up to be successful in their international endeavors. These efforts employed a much wider range of tools, with diplomatic elements at the forefront, and achieved enduring successes.

The distribution of power since the end of the Cold War, with one country so clearly dominant, has been a historical aberration. Yet our strategic choices have not, so far, used this interregnum of

American hegemony to advantage. Institutionalizing cooperation was an important and successful way of reducing the cost of governing the international order. Now, America is mostly sullen in refusing to accede to international institutions and treaties, even when they are manifestly in our interest—as with the Law of the Sea Treaty, for example, and its codification of the freedom of navigation so crucial for a maritime power.

Internationally, our country has been acting with disdain for other peoples' problems, crowing about our exceptionalism while taking too little responsibility for what our indifference fosters. We see this most clearly in Iraq, Syria, and Afghanistan, where our resources and resolve have been inadequate to our objectives. The gap between our rhetoric and our actions is leading to cynicism on the part of our fellow countrymen regarding the broader world and generating, in return, a sturdy cynicism on the part of the global audience toward America. Even long-term friends of our country are hedging their bets, questioning the reliability of our historic partnerships. Others are turning elsewhere for leadership because of the large and growing gap between what we say and what we do.

We see now an accelerating decline in the management of the state system. The results are:

- Russia has violated the borders of nearby nations, exercising veto authority over the diplomatic, economic, and security interests of nation states in Russia's "near abroad" and attempting to carve a recidivist sphere of influence that is out of step with modern international practice on sovereignty.

- China is doing the same, demanding veto authority over the rights of its neighbors in the South China Sea. This behavior follows a classical Chinese "tribute" model that demands deference from "lesser" nations in Beijing's sphere of interest.

- In the Middle East, two brands of violent jihadists attack the state system using religious affiliation:

  ○ The Sunni brand (Al Qaeda and associated movements) declared war on the West in the 1990s. More recently, ISIS has declared a caliphate, bulldozed the border between Iraq and Syria, and is still winning a war in the geopolitical heart of the Middle East. It is now striking outward, regionally and globally, exactly as it said it would do.

  ○ The Shia brand (Hezbollah, Hamas, and others supported by Iran) declared war on the United States in 1983, arms and trains terrorist organizations, acts as kingmaker in Lebanon, and across the Middle East supports the revolutionary cause it espouses, also challenging state legitimacy. Iranian negotiators have achieved a good outcome from the nuclear talks. The unfortunate aspects of that agreement were a result, in no small part, of the perception that the United States needed a deal more desperately than the Iranians and of the belief among all involved that America would not exercise a military option.

We under-invest in both our nonmilitary and military means of dealing with these problems. Our diplomatic corps is starved for managerial attention to increase its reach and abilities and is discouraged from taking initiative by the policy process in Washington. The American military is experiencing a slow diminishment of competence, capability, and proficiency in nuclear deterrence, decisive conventional combat, and irregular warfare as a result of budget malpractice, lack of consistent political clarity and direction, and organizational inattention to the core tasks of producing combat-ready forces.

Forty years into an all-volunteer military force, our broader society is losing sight of the necessity of maintaining a war-fighting military. There seems to be little understanding or appreciation outside the military for the risks associated with diverting attention in military units from the grim and demanding business of proficiency in combat. We are currently weighing our force down with ancillary requirements to such an extent that soldiering is an interruption of administrative duties. To use the lexicon of British naval historian Andrew Gordon's history of the Royal Navy's decline, we prefer regulators to rat-catchers. History has not been kind to militaries that lose focus on war-fighting.

Our defense enterprise also suffers from problems that we aren't worried enough about. Among these are:

- border security, which is distinct from immigration, and badly compromised by a conflation of the two issues;

- nuclear rearmament and proliferation, respectively, back in fashion for the saber-rattling Russians and expansive Chinese, and a grave risk for the Middle East in the aftermath of the Iranian treaty;

- incorporation into all military activity of the space and cyber domains in which we will unavoidably have to fight in the event of future conflict.

RELEARNING THE ART OF STRATEGY

So how do we right this ship? How do we correct our strategic course and reconstitute a less brittle international order? Understanding, of course, that a quest for perfection is quixotic, how do we ensure that we are not knocked off balance when the next unforeseen crisis strikes?

One of the central reasons our strategy has become so vapid is the tendency—especially evident in the President's National Security Strategy since the end of the Cold War—to list so many countries and issues that no genuine priorities are established. Rather than establishing principles for deciding which issues and events to devote effort toward, so-called strategy documents become Christmas trees festooned with ornaments. We understand the political pressures toward expansiveness; but the practice is an impediment to genuine understanding of our national purposes and how to attain them, which is the point of strategy. Rather than cataloguing every interest, strategy should consist of decision rules that allow for application to events as they unfold.

National security discussions also quickly telescope down to numbers and tactics; it gives the illusion of seriousness to appear to "get to the nitty-gritty." This is a mistake: appropriate force-structure numbers must be a derivative of what needs doing. Tactics are easy and relatively straightforward. Strategy is much harder, requiring consideration of a wide variety of factors and constant adjustment to circumstances as they develop. Moreover, tactical energy in a strategic vacuum is a recipe for disaster.

As Professor Colin Gray has written, "All strategy has to be about the consequences of threat and action." Strategy is a process, not an endpoint. It is a process of problem-solving in circumstances where much is outside one's ability to control (in physics terms, an open, complex system), placing a premium on learning and rapid adaptation to develop integrated ways of achieving essential ends. The role of strategy is to reduce uncertainty to the degree we can and to be prepared to respond even when we are surprised.

The strategic process starts with defined political ends: if you don't have those, then you can't have a strategy. Political ends can change, but they must be realistic and coherent to drive strategy. They set the levels of ambition for what will be attempted and drive the level of resourcing (revenue, military size, and national will) required to attain them. Acting strategically requires that political leaders make clear what they will stand for and what they will *not* stand for. We must mean what we say, to both allies and foes.

Political leaders who attempt to keep their options open by remaining vague or opaque about their ultimate ends actually limit their nation's ability to attain them and squander trust and resources in the execution—if their approach can be executed at all. Perhaps most importantly, confusion about the end state to be attained destroys trust that has been years in the making—and which is difficult to reconstitute. You can't "surge" trust. Growing and maintaining trust demands constant attention if we are to avoid the effect of entropy.

We need always to guard against the false confidence of predictability. In 1807, no one guessed that within a decade the Royal Navy would sail up the Chesapeake and burn Washington, DC; in 1907 no one guessed we would soon fight in Europe with gas masks and tanks and bombs dropped from the air. These examples make clear that the future is not foreseeable, however prescient we may think we are.

Given a reliably uncertain future, America cannot adopt one preclusive form of warfare. The paradox of war is that our enemies will always move against our perceived weakness. Thus our strategy must not—and must never—say what we will *not* do: no enemy should be reassured in advance that we won't employ ground troops, or that we will not fight beyond a certain date, or that we won't engage in certain types of fights.

A healthy military is a crucial component of restoring our national security. But it is not the totality. The military's role in the strategy process is to convey insights and lessons up the chain of command to political leaders and to wield deadly force to attain the nation's political objectives. Our military capability today needs to be woven, along with other elements of national power, into a strategy designed to succeed in the short term while buying time until we regain our fundamental political unity and will at home. Yet America's nonmilitary muscles have also atrophied, tilting the balance of our engagement with the world and shifting into military channels activities better performed by civilian departments.

With fifteen years at war since 9/11, we are long overdue in developing the ability to integrate the whole of our national security operations. Civilian departments are too weak to keep pace with the military's contributions in areas like capacity-building for friendly governments; the National Security Council process is unable to raise questions at the right level, solicit and incorporate differing views, and delegate the effort to monitor performance and rebalance our efforts. These continuing impediments require us to be realistic about what we can accomplish.

A STRATEGY OF SECURITY AND SOLVENCY

Economics are integral to military power. In fact, they are dispositive: no country has ever long retained its military power when its economic foundation faltered. Seen from a broader perspective, America's current fiscal situation is our central national security challenge. Our fiscal house is in disarray and we are on an unsustainable spending path. Even if interest rates remain at the current historically low rates, the end of this decade will see us paying more tax dollars to service our debt—interest paid to Riyadh, Moscow, and Beijing—than we have available to fund all of the Defense Department.

We are living far beyond our means, unable to summon the will to put our entitlement spending on a sustainable footing. Instead we squeeze discretionary government spending and compound the error by treating defense and domestic programs equally. Even those political platforms that envisage more robust defense spending fail to marry those aspirations with the revenue streams to pay for them or the political coalition to produce them on a sustained basis.

The failure to set (and be accountable for) national priorities is not only a grave political failing by our leaders; it amounts to intergenerational theft. Moreover, we appear to the world as incapable of governing ourselves, diminishing the inspirational power of the American order and increasing the real cost to us of maintaining that order.

Our national debt is the primary determinant of our strategic latitude. No national security strategy is possible if we fail to reduce our debt payments. The urgency of putting the country on a sound financial footing is thus paramount for our national security. As President Eisenhower said, "We must achieve both security and solvency." The two, in fact, are inseparable.

BURDEN SHARING

As we are not the only beneficiaries of the international order, we alone should not bear its security burdens. Popular fallacies abound that technology will do it all; that secretive special operations are sufficient; that allies will do the heavy lifting and dirty work; and that even if America opts out of tending the international order, it will continue to function in ways conducive to our interests. All of these beliefs are being disproven daily by global events, many with the grimmest possible consequences.

Those who oppose sustained international involvement because of its cost have the argument exactly wrong: only by coming together with allies and attending to the maintenance of the international order can we amass the resources necessary for the long-term management of our interests. Unilateralism may occasionally be necessary, when speed or secrecy require, but it is costly. It is also inconsistent historically with America's greatest achievements, when we led alliances of responsible nations in worthy causes.

Preserving an international order conducive to our interests becomes much more affordable when working with, and through, our allies. That means any strategy America adopts must, foremost, be ally-friendly. Allies have enduring, shared values with us, reflected through institutional structures. Alliances coalesce when we commit to solving common problems. They are an enormous asset for our country, demonstrating the breadth of our support and sharing the burden of our interests. These established relationships need restoring, and we need to draw more closely to our side both traditional and new allies who benefit from the American order. We must be able to rely on each other's commitment to build sufficient forces for the work at hand.

Our strategy must restore strengthened military ties with allies: NATO, Australia, Japan, South Korea, Middle Eastern nations (Jordan, Bahrain, the United Arab Emirates, Israel, Egypt, Saudi Arabia)—all the traditional allies who may now question our reliability. We ought also to create new alliances, further extending the circle of cooperation as American leaders set out to do following World War II. From India to Mexico to Vietnam, Brazil, and beyond, if America makes clear that we are ready to lead and willing to help, others may join. None will join if we continue our strategy-free approach.

In addition to allies, we need coalition partners. Rather than continue to operate as though countries that are not with us are against us—in the formulation made by President George W. Bush in the fraught days after 9/11—the right American approach would be to flip the arrow: those countries that are not against us are for us. The central difficulty we see in coalition relations is prioritizing our interaction with allies. We can't wait for perfect partners—nor are we a perfect partner. We seem to have lost the art of compromise with allies. Our tendency is to withhold cooperation until they do what we want, dismissing out of hand the validity of their objectives and the legitimacy of their interests, an approach that is ultimately isolating.

The core of building alliances must be that we say what we mean and do what we say: America must make no empty threats. Our partners must be able to count on us. And they need to understand our priorities. Yet we send confusing and contradictory signals by being unclear about the basis for our interactions.

Political leaders need to explain and defend the shared priorities driving our involvement. Our interests are a justifiable basis for cooperation, even when partners conduct their domestic policies in ways we may disapprove of. We need to recover the humility of understanding that we, also, conduct our domestic policies in ways partners disapprove of, and yet we are fortunate they cooperate with us on international objectives of mutual interest.

FORCE CHARACTERISTICS

We envision a strategy that plays to America's strengths. We will never be a country that speaks with one voice, or acts in unison, or in which the principal expertise in many crucial areas resides in government. The dynamism of our society exists beyond the Beltway, in the free markets and innovation centers of our civil society that adapt malleably to change. Washington will never be able to command civil society and match the decisiveness of authoritarian governments. But it can encourage, celebrate, and harness activity helpful to American causes.

More than any other nation, America can expand the competitive spaces in which our adversaries have to act: economic, diplomatic, geographic, informational, cultural, scientific, and more. Our strategic advantage lies in taking on our adversaries where they lack strength and seizing the initiative from them. Our reach extends far outside the realm of military operations and economic sanctions.

The priority challenges we would confront are: Russian belligerence, Chinese activities in the South China Sea, ISIS and Iranian aggressiveness, and drug-gang activity south of our border. Developing specific counterweights to these challenges would dictate the military alliances we develop. The goals would be to use the strength of our military alliances to help create constructive relations with Russia and China; to crush ISIS, Al Qaeda, and their franchises; to checkmate Iran's mischief; and to secure our borders.

Sustaining a world order fostering the interests of America and its allies will require maintaining strategic—including nuclear—deterrence, possessing decisive conventional capability, and making irregular warfare a core competency of our military. Deterring wars is, of course, preferable to fighting them. But deterrence only works when forces are adequate to the task.

We and our allies need the force structure to execute our commitments and carry out our war plans—and we no longer have it. The historic two-war standard ought to be, once again, the baseline force for a country with America's obligations, lest aggressors seek the advantage of striking while our forces are already engaged. It also merits mentioning that smaller numbers require an even higher quality of troops, at all levels, to include in its senior ranks.

Our national security strategy must also energize our intelligence community; with a smaller military and fewer overseas bases, we have less of a military shock-absorber than we once enjoyed. Successful military operations are more reliant than ever on fusion with intelligence, both for killing the enemy and for avoiding (to the degree possible) civilian casualties. Hence the need for the intelligence community to be our robust sentinels.

Another characteristic quality of a healthy military force is built-in, trained-in resilience, a force that can take surprises in stride and embrace uncertainty as part of war's nature. Resilience manifests itself in leaders who can respond to changing circumstances with creativity and innovation, because the enemy doesn't have to respect what we want. Resilience is also manifest in forces that are adaptable in their organization and equipment, agile in their speed of action, and employable across a wide spectrum of conflict.

These characteristics are seldom attained unless political leaders actively encourage sound military advice, even when it complicates their plans or contradicts their policies. The president ultimately gets the military advice he desires and deserves. As a country, we have not measured the ultimate costs of the outcomes we seek. Determining whether an outcome is worth the cost is a political judgment of enormous moral gravity. In our free society, only elected leaders are entrusted with those decisions—for which we need also to hold them accountable.

CONCLUSION

We have been profligate in pursuit of our national security because we haven't been acting strategically. Humility about the real world married to a fierce resolve to better protect America can address these problems and meet this need. We can recover a firm strategic stance in defense of our values by tending to the mechanisms—above all, the relationships—that ensure an international order conducive to American interests. Shaping the future, rather than merely accepting it, requires leadership. As President Truman, the great builder of the post-World War II order, said, "Men make history and not the other way around."

CHAPTER 11

REDEFINING ENERGY SECURITY

James O. Ellis Jr.

According to George Shultz, there are two key factors in negotiating a successful outcome in any endeavor. The first is to engage from a position of strength, when the timing is on your side. The second is to define and pursue your own current agenda, and not let your actions be driven by either your past or your opponent, lest you end up negotiating against yourself.

Today in the United States, for perhaps the first time in modern history, we find ourselves in a position of strength with respect to our energy system. Now is the optimal time for shaping and pursuing, both domestically and internationally, our energy goals. But we have grown so accustomed to domestic energy shortfall, with no alternative but to simply respond to external events, that we find ourselves with no energy agenda of our own.

It is time to redefine energy security and to define a comprehensive national energy security strategy. We need to understand and employ our new-found energy largesse in a framework that will guide our domestic and global engagement into the future. The next century of American energy will not be like the last.

Secretary Shultz often relates the story of meeting with President Eisenhower as a young member of his Council of Economic

---

I wish to acknowledge the constructive contributions made to this essay by both George P. Shultz and David Fedor.

Advisers. Eisenhower had warned that if the country were to rely on imports for more than a fifth of its petroleum needs, it would be in trouble. His prognostication alerted Shultz to the role of energy in our nation's vitality and also presaged the energy crises of the following decades. In 1969, Shultz led a cabinet-level task force on the growing energy security issue: a report was issued, hearings were held, but very little was done. The 1973 Arab Oil Boycott that followed—more or less what had been predicted—altered the energy landscape. By 1977, net energy imports hit 24 percent and imports from OPEC alone exceeded one-third of petroleum demand and over 18 percent of all US energy needs. But by that time, it was too late for a proactive strategic energy policy—the forced events of the energy crisis had already put the country on its back foot.

Since then, however, the situation has changed dramatically, largely due to three things: the deployment of a variety of better power generation technologies; hydraulic fracturing and horizontal drilling of domestic oil and gas; and improved efficiency throughout the economy. In 2014, just 16 percent of our country's net petroleum use was imported from OPEC. That is now less than 6 percent of our total energy consumption, putting OPEC behind the total energy supplied by, for example, the state of Pennsylvania (7 percent) and just ahead of Colorado (4 percent). It is also less than the share of our energy that comes from nuclear power (8 percent). Saudi Arabia, for its part, is responsible for about 2 percent of total US energy supply—on par with Arkansas, or just the growth alone in crude production from North Dakota over the past five years and equal to about what the United States produced from wind turbines last year.

The US energy situation today is by almost all accounts better than it has been for decades. So far, we have been the first and only country to successfully combine technology, business entrepreneurship, and our supportive legal and regulatory regimes to exploit abundant shale gas and shale oil resources: US overall petroleum production overtook Russia and Saudi Arabia in 2014 to become number one globally. Our fuel markets, refining, and trade infrastructure (even while currently challenged by a global environment of continued low prices) make us a lean and competitive supplier. Our energy business across sectors and fuels has a profound global reach. We lead on innovation in forms of energy both new and old. And as anyone who experienced Los Angeles basin smog in the 1980s can attest, the energy efficiency of our economy and improvements in environmental performance of our vehicles and power plants is breathtaking. We operate the largest carbon-free power generation fleet in the world, adding to it daily through new technologies. In sum, our newfound energy abundance offers the incoming administration a chance for something that no others in recent history have had: the opportunity to pause, absent the clamoring pressures of an energy crisis, and dispassionately reflect on our country's longer-term energy priorities.

It is tempting to ignore the opportunity, to relax after decades of lurching from crisis to crisis. But the fact is that our country today does not have a true energy strategy, and we have not had one for years. Even omnibus efforts such as the 2005 Energy Policy Act are more a collection of broad philosophies, loose ends, and pet interests than a comprehensive national posture on a defining issue.

We have taken a haphazard approach to energy, tilting from one issue-of-the-day to the next: from price controls to reducing "petro-state" import dependency, from domestic energy industry jobs to the environment. As each issue comes to the fore, it dominates the others at the expense of a comprehensive and systematic long-term energy strategy. Many of our greatest energy successes have, arguably, come in spite of our attempts at national policy, or at least as unintended consequences.

Early government investment in research and development (R&D) helped to seed the market, and was an absolutely necessary precursor, but fracking ultimately became economical and widespread largely due to the commendably dogged pursuits in the field by one businessman trying to improve the value of his cheaply acquired acreage. Many reasonable compromise efforts at improving energy-using products have borne fruit—vehicle fuel economy standards and emission standards, for example—but no one in the newly created Federal Energy Administration, itself a reaction to the 1973 oil crisis, foresaw the abrupt flattening of nationwide energy demand growth as industry adjusted production practices in creative and unexpected ways to reduce energy input needs. (According to energy economist Jim Sweeney, today our economy uses just six thousand BTUs of energy to create one dollar of GDP, versus fourteen thousand BTUs for that same dollar in 1973, an improvement of 57 percent.)

Meanwhile, ends-oriented federal programs to champion the deployment of certain energy technologies over others have had a spotty record at best. Some have produced new energy supplies (the subsidy of renewables and starch-based biofuels, for example) and some have not (the coal-to-liquid fuels program, carbon capture and sequestration, and cellulosic biofuels), but all have been expensive. Moreover, these government efforts have been far surpassed in scale and impact by the market responding to state-by-state power sector deregulation through the widespread deployment of natural gas turbine generation facilities.

Technological improvement through R&D has been the one clear bright spot, and an area in which federal research dollars have helped leverage similar private funding. But even those policies have been boom-and-bust, closely linked to the similarly volatile energy commodity prices that technology in itself has yet to solve.

Out passivity toward taking control of our energy destiny is not reflective of how America generally creates and conducts policy in other areas. Today, there is an unprecedented opportunity to do better. But this is not a call for an energy Apollo Program— an attractive conceit on the surface but ultimately irrelevant to the nature of our broader energy goals. Instead, we must recognize that we have been granted new global opportunities for engagement—as a reliable and competitive energy power—and that, as a result, we already are beginning to shoulder new responsibilities, many still indistinct.

So, what must be considered in defining a proactive, domestically beneficial, internationally competitive, and geopolitically effective energy security strategy for the next hundred years?

DOMESTIC ENERGY NEEDS

Our first priority in energy seems obvious, as it has heretofore dominated our thinking about energy. Energy supply security means that energy is always available (even in times of duress), that it is reliable (not prone to sudden disruption, whether intentional or accidental), resilient (able to recover quickly when it is interrupted), and affordable (both in the personal and macroeconomic sense, including price shocks).

Domestic or North American regional energy independence, a goal espoused by many, helpfully contributes to some of these elements of energy security. Our combined North American energy relationships in particular should be explicitly recognized and supported as a global model of competitiveness, diversity, dependability, and constructive regulation. Moreover, that shared competitiveness improves the broader economic viability of our closely linked economies against trade bloc competitors abroad. But "independence" in itself is limited in effectiveness and counterproductive to many other national goals. Energy independence means that US factories and homes would stay supplied if all borders were to be shut down during a conflict, but it does not mean that our expeditionary military forces—or our allies and trading partners—would be similarly taken care of. Energy independence helps with one side of our balance of trade but, given global fuel markets, it does not always mean lower prices for US consumers, nor does it optimize the value of local energy resource types or the refining and generation infrastructure on which the viability of our nation's energy companies depends.

For example, energy-independent Norwegian consumers today pay just as much more for gasoline when oil prices rise as we always have, despite their position as significant net oil exporters. And at an economy-wide scale, our energy industry is actually a significant beneficiary of petroleum trade—with Mexico, for instance, where crude is imported, refined here using our more advanced infrastructure, and then exported back to Mexican consumers as diesel and gasoline, an export worth over $20 billion annually and employing American workers in the meantime. Moreover, independence does little for reliability or resiliency. A winter storm can shut down power to the US Northeast no matter where the coal or natural gas comes from, and cyber-attacks do not discriminate on the national origin of electrons. One could argue that a broad-based web of domestic and international supply could be designed such that more, not fewer, points of energy trade and infrastructure connection would improve system-wide reliability and flexibility and make it easier to withstand shocks, be they geopolitical, meteorological, technical, or human.

Rather than seeking strict energy independence, it is far more prudent to invest our current energy dividend into creating a robust, diverse, competitive, redundant, and resilient generation and distribution system in order to improve our nation's energy security over the long term. All else equal, being able to trade among a portfolio of fuels, power generation technologies, private firms, regional suppliers, and resource bases ultimately increases our flexibility when we need it. Healthy domestic energy production is a valuable part of preserving our options because it reduces absolute reliance on any single trading partner.

When correctly managed against fragility, a network is more robust the more nodes that connect within it. It is just as important therefore that we continue to build strong and diverse global energy trading relationships—and maintain the markets, institutions, and infrastructure needed to support them—so that we do not end up isolating ourselves and becoming the ones at risk of being disrupted. We must think of ourselves as market-makers, and not merely as price-takers. The pursuit of energy independence, when expressed through efforts at energy isolationism, including the restriction of exports, actually serves to reduce our influence and options and hold us back, through "self-imposed sanctions" (to use Alaska Senator Lisa Murkowski's phrase).

Another step we would take toward long-term domestic energy security is to step up investment in energy technology, both those inventions that seem promisingly near at hand (but are not quite ready to deliver on their own) and the very risky but potentially game-changing options on the horizon. This is not a call for a blank check, or for the government to get directly involved in commercialization. But it is an acknowledgement that the breathing space afforded to us now by the investments in R&D of yesterday—hydraulic fracturing, for example, or efficient vehicles and LED light bulbs—gives us an opportunity to think over a longer time horizon to support what will come next. Much of what we put our research money into will ultimately not become viable, but there is intrinsic value in improving the stock of available technology options so that those we do eventually use are the most economical and highest performance ones possible. Long term R&D investment in generation, distribution, and utilization is essential for our continued energy leadership, innovative achievement, and economic success.

GLOBAL ENGAGEMENT

While the domestic energy security implications of our energy dividend will take time to flower, new avenues for US global engagement are already available to us. Energy-exporting superpowers have throughout their history been tempted to use their dominance as a weapon. For us, energy is instead a tool to support allies and positively influence newly diversified markets with global effect. Now that we are no longer relegated to defining ourselves simply as victims of the global energy regime, what will be the US energy doctrine?

First, with our own domestic needs largely accounted for, we should use our energy to help our partners and allies. This does not mean, for example, that everyone in Europe needs to be buying American LNG. Russia is a major low-cost supplier and it would not be in our long-term interest to use natural gas as leverage to kick Russia while it is down economically, especially in a perceived tit-for-tat response to Russia's past actions with its own neighbors. But a diversified market, with US participation, does allow us to be a credible energy alternative in parts of the world where we have previously had little to offer.

The plight of the Baltic States in relying on Russian natural gas and electric grids is well-known. Less known is that when Lithuania recently began operation of the region's first small floating LNG import facility, even with only a portion of the terminal's capacity contracted, the country's Russian-negotiated wholesale natural gas prices dropped by 23 percent overnight. The difference between monopoly and choice is a significant one. Ukraine has reduced its own reliance on Russian natural gas by half and Bulgaria is similarly interested in access to US supplies. We cannot supply the world, but even a marginal contribution can make a difference in shaping market forces and national behaviors. It gives us an option to neutralize an existing geopolitical weapon without needing to use military force. We should therefore seek to establish relationships, redefine markets, and create the trading infrastructure in regions around the world where we might be able to make a difference—focusing on those areas where we can use energy to deter rather than encourage conflict.

Our ability to engage constructively with allies and trading partners is not limited to those parts of the world facing sovereign threats. Japan and South Korea, apart from their domestic nuclear power industries, are both almost completely reliant on imports for their energy supplies, a fact for which they pay dearly. Closer to home, Mexico is undergoing a surge in demand for electricity and natural gas as recent substantial reforms take hold and its manufacturing economy surges. We already supply over a quarter of Mexico's natural gas and that figure will rise with the development of new pipelines and power plants to use it. Our existing energy commerce with Canada, across oil, gas, coal, biomass, and electricity, is already one of the largest global energy trades, worth over $100 billion annually. United States energy exports present a fresh opportunity to deepen our mutually beneficial relationships with these friends and neighbors, and deserves far more than perfunctory treatment.

Of course, additional global engagement on energy is not entirely selfless. There are clear economic benefits at home. Beyond the obvious examples of increased petroleum fuel exports, a US global energy doctrine should also recognize the fundamental role of our energy technology and operational know-how. Our world-leading oil production majors and field service companies already act as ad hoc ambassadors in regions where their influence may well run ahead of that of the state itself in the value of the innovation and performance they offer. American power plant technology vendors occupy a similar industry-leading position. The International Energy Agency estimates that global power sector investment alone through 2040 will exceed $21 trillion, increasing global capacity by 80 percent. New breakthroughs in adjacent technologies in the renewable energy sector, grid-scale storage, and grid operational or cyber-defense technologies will be similarly sought after. The United States—through both multinational firms and concerted government efforts—can claim credit for successfully spreading civilian nuclear power technologies, and contracts, across the globe. As other new generation sources, including promising nuclear technologies, gradually emerge, how will the United States continue to maintain a competitive and influential international energy role?

In any such calculus, there are two questions to answer: (1) do we have the capability to competitively engage? and (2) do we choose to do anything about it? As the answer to the former increasingly becomes affirmative, across a range of energy forms and technologies, the second question also demands a formulated response. What should be the role of the state in each of these realms? We are not China, strongly coordinating outward investment and tying it closely to geopolitical aims, nor are we a laissez faire libertarian utopia. The recent debates over the reauthorization of the US Export-Import Bank speak to the difficulty in articulating a meaningful and economically beneficial response to these new opportunities.

There are illuminating models from other sectors worth considering. In information technology, for example, early US dominance in software, chips, servers, and networking equipment and architecture led to its technologies being adopted globally as de facto and, later, negotiated standards. Sometimes controversially, that dominance has also allowed the country to exploit those technologies for national security purposes. Similarly, in banking, the strength of American financial institutions and the centrality of the US dollar itself have helped give us an advantaged role in the global financial sphere. Today, when the United States wishes to apply economic sanctions, for example, those actions are animated not just by the reach of our trade ties, but also by our ability to effectively monitor and control financial asset transfers that almost ubiquitously clear through American organs—peace through our strengths, with or without force.

With energy, the United States has already shown a values-oriented appetite to use its influence in that sector to help define norms for safety and responsible environmental performance. Again, in nuclear power, we effectively used our primacy in the international supply and technology chain to improve global standards not only in design, licensing, and operational safety, but also in oversight of the nuclear fuel cycle and related fissile material counter-proliferation efforts. Today, consider the Arctic, an area whose strategic importance to the United States will only grow. Shell has, for a variety of reasons, recently announced a withdrawal from its multiyear and multibillion-dollar efforts to explore for oil off the coast of Alaska. Many in the environmental community saw this as a victory. The sad truth is that Shell's withdrawal means that the United States has lost an opportunity to use its vast experience and high standards to help avoid catastrophe in the precarious Arctic environment. Gazprom recently announced the 10 millionth barrel of production from its Arctic Prirazlomnoye field off the Russian north shore. These efforts continue, without the "compare and contrast" opportunity that would be offered by a modern, safe, and environmentally secure American initiative.

A final opportunity for redoubled US international engagement on the back of our energy dividend is our ability to substantively revisit our ethical stance toward energy poverty. Twenty percent of people globally have no access to electricity; for a billion more, what access they have is erratic. This means that a farmer cannot reliably run a pump to irrigate crops, medical personnel cannot keep life-saving hospital equipment on line, and an entrepreneur cannot keep computers running in an office without relying on an expensive generator.

At the low end of the economic development spectrum, even given improvement in energy efficiency, the statistics are clear: if a country wants to increase its GDP per capita from $100 to $1,000, it needs a ten-fold increase in the supply of energy. As we consider the next American energy century, it is worth looking back at our own energy development. Historian and commentator Vaclav Smil in a 2004 essay noted that the typical American household at the turn of the twenty-first century had access to more than sixty times the energy capacity than it did in 1900, and at a small fraction of the cost. If you include cars, the numbers are even more remarkable, with that same suburban household wielding the power equivalent of "a 19th century landlord employing 3,000 workers and 400 large draft horses." Yet today, the richest 10 percent of the world's population claims 45 percent of all energy, while the poorest half are left with just 10 percent. The opportunity for improvement in global energy access is staggering.

At a time of uncertain public support, energy can also help give new meaning to our international aid efforts. In Africa and Asia, many women not only spend hours each day collecting firewood, their use of those primitive fuels actually harms them and their families. The World Health Organization estimates that indoor air pollution from cooking results in nearly two million deaths annually, which could be avoided through the use of much cleaner commercial fuels such as LPG or natural gas. Though not a perfect analogy, the robust American agriculture industry—including both the export of surplus US crops to famine regions and the spread of American agricultural and seed technologies to improve crop yields—offers one model on how to leverage a competitive US advantage into formation of a domestic constituency to support durable aid policies. Though there is no easy answer to this issue, it is important enough that we should explore how our broad energy strengths could be applied here as well.

The United States is exceptional for how its powerful economy, its national security assurances, and its very democratic values have long been tools to create and sustain a web of strong relationships across the globe. It is time to add energy to that mix.

ENERGY PRIORITIES

Finally, we have to acknowledge that abundance changes the nature of our domestic conversations on energy—our collective priorities and values around energy affordability, equity, and the environment. As has been the theme of these thoughts, new choices give us new space to maneuver; but we have to define the basic course. Much of the current domestic discourse over energy priorities has taken the tone of a political campaign. But as Shultz has noted, campaigning is fundamentally an act of division. We have unfortunately grown used to unending campaigns and wide and deep divides. Strategy, on the other hand, is the act of making things nonpartisan (as distinct from bipartisan). Energy strategy must be an inclusive act of governance.

The elephant in the room today is carbon dioxide emissions, contributing to global warming. This is an issue with broad consequences, one that offers no clear or painless path to success. As we consider how our collective values around global warming should influence our energy choices, any trade-offs against our other central energy objectives should be supported by elucidating relative social priorities. At the core, to what degree do we accept higher prices, or potentially reduced reliability, in order to achieve an increased measure of decarbonization? This is a judgment call. But it can be informed by honest and largely objective evaluations of the question.

One example helps illustrate the potential risk of a single issue —or any single favored technological solution—dominating what should be a comprehensive approach. As global warming has animated the minds of many (though not all) Americans, wind and solar power have been held out by advocates as particularly desirable solutions, resulting in a number of targeted subsidies and regulations. Renewables have quickly grown, though their share of domestic power generation remains in the low single digits. Meanwhile, existing nuclear power plants, which represent nearly 20 percent of American electricity needs, are suddenly at risk of closure due in part to electricity market distortions brought on by renewables policies. Something is wrong here. If our social priority is to reduce greenhouse gases or air pollution, and the result of our actions is to threaten the viability of our largest source of zero-emission power, we have not delivered a comprehensive agenda.

A similar strain of current domestic energy politics seeks to restrict the use of the hydraulic fracturing and horizontal drilling responsible for delivering much of our current energy abundance, driven by a concern that air or water pollution from elements of the process risk harming human health. This is a valid concern.

But a comprehensive judgment should evaluate it against both our social priorities and our real-world alternatives.

One objective truth here is that cheap natural gas, the result of domestic fracking, has led US power generators to switch to it over coal in droves. More power is now generated in this country by (relatively cleaner burning) natural gas than by our traditional coal mainstay. Another relevant fact is that domestic air pollution from coal-fired power plants, by multiple estimates, kills more than ten thousand Americans annually. There is, as yet, no such data showing commensurate direct harm to human health from fracking. When exploring and assessing values-based energy priorities, we as a society have yet to create satisfactory tools or processes to fairly evaluate and pursue them, especially where our best options may not be immediately apparent.

To this end, an overarching uncertainty is the ability of the existing institutional framework for energy in this country to optimally deliver on comprehensive technological, societal, and environmental priorities, given that the framework itself is an organic and largely ad hoc outgrowth of our country's regional energy history.

States dominate some realms of energy policy through their traditional role as regulators of monopoly power utilities, though their powers are not evenly distributed. California, for example, has been able to be the de facto regulatory body for national vehicle pollution and even fuel efficiency standards due in part to its market size. Elsewhere, groups of states have banded together to form regulatory compacts and interstate agreements on issues ranging from oil pipeline safety to carbon dioxide trading. A host of federal bodies engages with the states in sometimes poorly defined ways that rely on drawn-out court cases or negotiations to resolve, be it esoteric terms of interstate wholesale power transfers or far-reaching subsidies and mandates to rebuild trillions of dollars in power generation infrastructure. Institutional relationships are adversarial by design and seem to be incapable of producing even collaborative, much less consensual, outcomes.

Energy policy and management in the federal government itself are hardly straightforward. The Department of Energy (DOE) handles energy statistics, funds energy research and a network of national labs, and sets the tone for the nation's energy posture, but its budget reflects its main job: to secure and manage the country's nuclear weapons stockpile facilities. A collection of federal regulatory agencies, from across departments, sets important energy performance and safety standards. In recent years, an increasingly athletic Environmental Protection Agency has emerged as perhaps the most influential, and contested, federal energy body through its expansive employment of congressionally granted jurisdiction over the nation's air and water.

Meanwhile, the nascent task of global energy engagement is shared between DOE and the State Department. The problem here is not that this Pythagorean arrangement does not keep the trains running on time, but that overall responsibility is diffused. No one body is in charge, which helps explain why we lack any comprehensive agenda. As the system stands today, it is unclear which entities would be able to deliver the domestic energy supply or outward-looking global energy security strategies described above. Delivering on a new American energy doctrine may well involve goals that are broader than any one agency. Getting there would require not just the identification and articulation of priorities, but also a responsibility-identifying road map—including any necessary structural reforms.

As to road maps, it is important to recognize that a grandiose goal or pledge is not the same thing as a strategy. A numerical target, by itself, is a sort of binding ideology—it can be used to justify choices that otherwise would not make sense. Instead, it is more useful to focus on agreeing on what worthwhile concrete actions can be undertaken today so that they can be prototyped, tested, and improved. Statistics are a useful way to help evaluate progress; actions are what effect change, so they should remain the focus of negotiation.

Given these challenges of governance, it is viscerally enticing to appeal to the free market for answers. It is the correct starting principle. Many economists, for example, have advocated eloquently for a revenue-neutral carbon tax as the ideal tool to address the negative externalities of carbon dioxide emissions: incorporate the real social costs of pollution across the economy, and let the market (i.e., individual choices) decide the cheapest way to deliver results, all the while returning any new government revenues back to the American people to reduce household costs and avoid the unnecessary side effect of an enlarged public bureaucracy. According to analysts, it would "level the playing field" for energy as far as global warming is concerned, and with less pain than the alternatives.

Surprisingly, the idea has failed to catch on politically, despite being embraced by some of the nation's largest energy firms. One tension may be the reality that energy is not a completely free market in the United States to begin with. Government interventions are the bedrock of some sectors—the monopoly regulated utility model, for example—or have otherwise become ingrained in the continued viability of others. Leveling the playing field—while a reasonable goal and therefore worth pursuing—will change the status quo in potentially unpredictable ways, even if the overall situation is improved in the end. The other challenge facing the carbon tax is that it has not been given a neutral airing before the electorate. Interest groups from all sides have hijacked the climate issue as a vehicle for ulterior interests. People need to feel trust that the same would not happen here. But these are soluble problems. More optimistic recent opinion polls do suggest that the public is embracing the concept faster than their political representatives, so there may be catching up to do in Washington and the state capitols.

To the extent that governance is about "how to get things on people's minds," the revenue-neutral carbon tax, like many other potentially attractive energy policies, demands leadership if it is to be embraced by the industries and people who would ultimately have to pay it. Though the challenges here are real, a motivated leader should not use that as a reason to shirk from them but rather to ask, "If not this, then what?" A decision not to act, or to maintain a flawed status quo—where a current vacuum of leadership on the issue is rapidly filling with the detritus of others' policy agendas—is still a decision. The climate issue is housed firmly in American minds and in geophysical realities. It will not fade away.

However we choose to articulate and prioritize our national energy priorities, the process must be seen as fair and reasonable. When we are dealing with decisions and investments that are long-term in nature, it is essential that our chosen course transcend politics and survive across administrations. Our long-term interest is not served by one faction exerting a temporary position of strength over another, only to be later reversed. Leadership will require integrity, something that underlies our scientific, academic, corporate, and governmental processes when they are at their best. Underlying integrity is openness, honesty, and the ability to have those crucial conversations—and confrontations— that must be a part of this continuing journey.

In addressing our energy circumstances, we as Americans find ourselves in a place we have never been with opportunities we have never had and choices we have never before been offered. We have a fleeting window to redefine energy security in terms beyond our own domestic needs and embrace the leadership possibilities and imperatives in creating a global framework within which we and our partners can prosper economically, progress societally, and participate in shared energy security. It is breathtaking how far we have come (as is the nature of the challenges to which we have risen) over the past century of American energy history. It is our good fortune in this century to now find ourselves with the strength to be able to redefine energy security for the next.

Editor's Comment

It seems that Jim Ellis is onto a big idea: the time is right for finding a path to a new national energy strategy. As I see it, what we ultimately want is something that gives us three things: plentiful, low-cost energy for our economy; secure energy so that we don't face the risk of hostile cut-offs from abroad (think of the Arab Oil Boycott of 1973); and energy that does as little damage as possible to our environment—the air we breathe and the environment we help create. Against these objectives, the current moment presents relatively new and outstanding possibilities.

So within that neutral strategic framework, let me use my editorial privilege to fill in two key concrete policy measures that I am convinced need to populate it—both of which should be carried out narrowly, and neither of which need be ideological.

The first is strong and sustained support for energy R&D. New technologies and methods, in considerable part from past energy R&D investments (an overused word in politics, but appropriate here), have given us a plentiful and secure supply of oil and gas, particularly when buttressed by our energy connections with our neighbors, Canada and Mexico. And with cheap natural gas replacing coal, the overall effect on our environment is quite positive. All of this is within our borders, so we have a positive economy, positive national security, and a positive contribution to the environment. What's not to like?

But more advancements are needed—some of which are nearer at hand, others on the horizon. As Jim alluded, I have spent considerable time on the energy issue since my time in office up to the present in my roles with the research programs at Stanford and MIT. So I am fortunate to see first-hand the creative work that goes on at universities and elsewhere. Over the last few years, with high oil and gas prices, the largest-ever scientific and engineering effort has gone into energy research—with visible and important results. Solar and wind energy are now competitive on a cost basis and, with the prospect of large-scale storage, their intermittency problems could diminish. Storage developments also mean there will be some insurance against cyber or other attacks on our grid. On that count, I'm also optimistic on the prospect for small modular nuclear reactors, which could be revolutionary in every way.

Always in the past, these energy R&D efforts surged when oil and gas prices were high and subsided when prices came down. This time, we need a policy that keeps R&D efforts strong, and that policy needs to be accompanied by something that levels the playing field in terms of deployment.

This brings me to my second point.

Right now, we see a wide variety of subsidies, mandates, and special arrangements across the energy spectrum. They will not get us where we want to go. There is a simple and attractive alternative, and one that also gets at the carbon emission free-rider problem among countries.

A revenue-neutral carbon tax could accompany the repeal of all subsidies (as is practically feasible) and simply make every source of energy take on its full cost, including the cost of putting carbon into the atmosphere. It could be made revenue-neutral by having all the funds put into an easily identifiable pool—perhaps one administered by an existing trusted agency such as the Social Security Administration—and then distributed to individuals.

I speak with economists on the pros and cons of various potential policy design details, and their positions vary; the option favored by both the late Gary Becker and myself is simply to refund every cent collected in an even amount to everyone with a Social Security number. Meanwhile, a border tax on imported goods, commensurate with their embedded carbon content and feeding into that same carbon fund for use by US citizens, would protect our competitiveness and give other countries a reason to sign on with a similar measure of their own—which is, after all, the whole point. The key principle with such an economically impactful measure would be to keep it simple, so that everyone understands what they are signing on to and so that it is harder to tinker with over time (just as Alaska has managed to do with its straightforward oil fund dividend, but at which the various complex carbon cap-and-trade systems around the world have consistently failed). Energy requires enormous investments, and investment needs predictability. So I'm not surprised that even our major energy producers tend to like the revenue-neutral carbon tax. Something is happening here.

As Jim Ellis wrote, the climate issue is not going away—far better to be equipped with a respectable policy agenda of one's own to work from than negotiating against another's playbook.

GPS

CHAPTER 12

DIPLOMACY IN A
TIME OF TRANSITION

James E. Goodby

The international system is changing and no one knows what it will look like when equilibrium is finally reached, perhaps decades from now. Already, nation-states find it necessary to share power with regional or global organizations. Adversarial relations between governments and major economic units have existed for a long time. Now, the relationship takes the form of power-sharing in order to maximize benefits to each side.

Nationalism is still a potent force, and is likely to remain so. But its appearance on the international stage draws a strong response from other nations and international organizations. The effect is to reduce the benefits that the practitioners of aggressive nationalism might expect to receive from a globalized economy were they to curb their nationalistic ambitions. An anti-war effect exercised by the impossibility of one nation enriching itself by seizing assets of another was predicted on the eve of World War I.[1] Is anything different in our time? Judging by Vladimir Putin's actions in Ukraine, evidently not. So the power-seeking remnants of an earlier age will likely be a part of the international scene for a long time to come and aggressive use of military force will remain a threat to peace and security.

BETWEEN TWO WORLDS

This points to the need to create a new "global commons," in the sense that a common response to global challenges is essential to avoid catastrophe for the human race. The structures created at the end of World War II and during the Cold War remain useful in bolstering world order. But they were mainly Western structures. Now a regime-building process is underway in Asia and it already has produced organizations that can be used either to encourage or to thwart the creation of a true global commons. Regional institutions with real power are probably an improvement over unbridled nationalism. But a world of competing regional communities, each dominated by a single hegemon, would not necessarily be more peaceful than is the current system.

Nor would such a world deal more effectively with global existential threats to humanity than the current system. Climate change, water scarcity, nuclear devastation, and pandemics ultimately require a global response. Regional groupings, if linked in a cooperative fashion, could manage these existential threats, and that, perhaps, should be the near-term goal of order-building diplomacy. A global society with real clout is not likely to emerge for decades.

Another feature that defines contemporary international relations shows how inadequate the word "international" really is in conceptualizing what is happening to the system. In contrast to the state-centered system created by a top-down wielding of power by national governments, the emerging global system contains a large people-to-people element that wields power across state boundaries.

The empowerment of citizens through the ability to communicate and acquire information instantaneously has enormous potential for good or ill. Crowd-sourcing can provide answers to complex questions and monitor the implementation of treaties by national governments. The ability to draw together hundreds or thousands of people in a common reaction to events is a powerful tool. Whether this ability is exercised in a constructive manner depends on factors that transcend technology. It will clearly be a world very different from that in which statecraft has operated for centuries, a world truly in systemic transition, with elements of the old and new contending in a way that promotes complexity rather than simplicity.

THE SECRETARY OF STATE AND THE
PRESIDENT IN AMERICAN STATECRAFT

For this section, I interviewed George P. Shultz at the Hoover Institution. Secretary of state for six years under President Ronald Reagan, he reflected on the relations between the president and the secretary of state in the conduct of foreign policy.

Secretary Shultz said the first rule he followed was to be clear about who was elected and who was not. He always emphasized that he did not have a policy: US foreign policy was the president's policy. Key to their relationship was trust. The president knew that he could rely on his secretary of state for honest advice and careful implementation of the president's foreign policy. Shultz, and those he dealt with, came to understand that Reagan's word was meticulously upheld by the president and that he was consistent in his dealings. Soviet leaders learned that they could deal with President Reagan. He and Shultz shared the view that George Kennan, author of the containment strategy, had espoused: over time, the Soviet Union would change, given a strong and consistent American policy of containment. The status quo, nurtured by détente, need not be the preferred US long-term objective.

Shultz said that strategic thinking was encouraged in the Reagan administration through twice-weekly private meetings with the president in which they avoided decision-making and looked over the horizon at issues that needed more thought. Shultz also set aside time for himself, to ponder American strategic objectives and assess whether the United States had achieved those.

As regards principles of statecraft, Shultz said, first, that strength and diplomacy must go hand-in-hand. Strength not used to secure an objective loses its meaning. Diplomacy without strength behind it is feckless.

A second cardinal principle was that a global diplomacy was essential. The United States needs a global involvement all the time. In following those precepts, Shultz found it necessary to develop a relationship of trust and confidence with leaders in all parts of the world. Only in that way could frank conversations be conducted that would point to solutions to issues as they arose.

Speaking of governance in the area of external relations, Shultz spoke of alternative ways of analyzing issues and making decisions. The one he thought produced better decisions is where presidents rely on cabinet officers and senior sub-cabinet officials for advice and the National Security staff serves the principals of the National Security Council. The alternative of relying primarily on White House staff deprives the president of the best advice available from the major departments and their career personnel. It results in less consultation with the cabinet and the departments and limits the ability of presidents to receive broadly based advice on key issues.

Shultz also spoke of the need for spending time with members of Congress. A good reason for this is that they have worthwhile ideas. Another is that ratification of treaties goes more smoothly if senators have been involved and understand the issues. Shultz also observed that it is hard to build an A-team in government when the confirmation process has become so elaborate and unpredictable.

THE DEPARTMENT OF STATE AS AN INSTITUTION

To grasp the enormous systemic changes that have occurred since the rise of the United States as a global superpower at the end of World War II, consider the recommendations of the Hoover Commission on the conduct of foreign affairs published in 1949.[2]

The commission, chaired by former president Herbert Hoover, was established by Congress to review the operations of the executive branch and make recommendations for improvement of its organization. President Truman sent a special message to Congress on Reorganization of the State Department on March 4, 1949.[3] He asked for four more assistant secretary of state positions "to permit the Department to organize its principal activities on a geographic basis." Truman also stressed the importance "strongly recommended by the Commission on Organization of the Executive Branch of the Government, *of clarifying the lines of responsibility and authority within the Executive Branch.*"

In recent years conventional wisdom has been that instead of vesting responsibility for important diplomatic activities in the State Department's line bureaus, special offices or "czars" should be created. If one looked at the State Department's telephone directory in 2015, one could find at least twenty such special offices.[4] This practice does not clarify the lines of responsibility and authority within the executive branch. Moreover, the idea of concentrating the principal activities of the State Department in its major bureaus, as advocated by the Hoover Commission, is undermined by peeling off important projects and handing them to persons or offices that typically are ad hoc and temporary. The expertise necessary for the successful conduct of diplomacy can only be developed by a sustained effort to recruit, train, and consciously assign personnel to a succession of increasingly complex and responsible positions.

Obviously, the challenges the United States now faces are very different from those the Hoover Commission saw in the aftermath of World War II. But in at least one way, there are similarities. The Hoover Commission reported:

> The State Department, since the war, has at all levels been too much concerned with "details" and not enough with "policy." The Secretary-Under Secretary top command is

overburdened by being drawn down into participation in too many daily decisions with the consequence that the entire Department lives day-to-day, and policies tend to be determined in terms of short-range decisions.

The first step in considering the reorganization of the State Department in the second decade of the twenty-first century should be to identify priority challenges. Bearing in mind that the international system today consists of remnants of the old and emerging features of the new, approaches to policy and application of resources will necessarily be complex.

CHALLENGES OLD AND NEW

This complexity is underscored by several issues that are features of a new global system:

- The long-standing state system for bringing order to the world is under pressure globally.
- The security and economic commons built up over several decades in the twentieth century is at risk everywhere and in many places no longer exists.
- The process of governance is changing rapidly and the advance of technology underlying this development suggests that this pressure will only intensify with time.
- Private groups empowered by technology can damage the coherence needed for effective governance.

Challenges that have been episodically present in the state system for centuries now appear simultaneously in large areas of the globe:

- State borders are being challenged in Europe, the Middle East, and Asia.
- The dispersion of sovereignty away from states has left national governments less able to be the main engines of action in the international system.

- Horizontal ideological solidarity encouraged by the communications revolution presents a threat to the border-defined states system.

- The re-entry of religious extremism into interstate relations threatens states and their ability to govern over diversity.

The first category of issues—new challenges that cannot be handled well by reliance only on conventional diplomacy—requires rethinking of the American agenda and how governance should adjust to manage the new environment. The second category—familiar challenges to the states system and the reason that system was created in the first place—requires a change in the way Washington conducts its international business.

A third category of challenge is the threat to humanity posed by climate change, water scarcity, nuclear weapons, and pandemics. The challenge that existential threats like these pose is whether states can cooperate in a sustained fashion to roll back or contain the threats. By moving rapidly to create a coalition of nations dedicated to meeting existential threats, the states system will position itself to better meet the exigencies of an emerging global system in which individual states are not, and cannot be, the supreme actors. This consideration is extremely important for the future development of structures of governance.

REGIONAL DIPLOMACY

Regional diplomacy is becoming a higher priority for statecraft than it has been in the past. This is so not only for economic and security reasons, the traditional motivators of regional cooperation, but also because some existential threats require at least regional cooperation, if not global cooperation. For example, climate change will produce water shortages in some parts of the world and regional cooperation can help to deal with this. Climate change will also generate migrations away from equatorial regions toward more hospitable climes. This flow of migrants will dwarf what has recently been seen in Europe and the Middle East. Again, if states can find a way to cooperate on a regional basis in dealing with this challenge, the states system will be strengthened. If not, populations will unite to erase borders and global chaos will prevail until some new form of governance can be devised.

EXECUTIVE-LEGISLATIVE RELATIONS

The complexity of these issues requires constant, timely consultation between the executive branch and the Congress. Many of the primary issues today have a large domestic component. The Hoover Commission saw the need for close consultation but the separation of powers was more pronounced and unbridgeable in the 1940s than it can be today. Even so, the commission recognized a new role for Congress. Here is what it said:

> The constitutional doctrine of separation of powers between the executive and legislative branches results in a duality of authority over foreign affairs which complicates the machinery of Government in that area, especially in contrast with the machinery of countries operating under the parliamentary system of government. . . .
>
> Recent events have changed the situation and made the Congress a much more significant and regular participant in foreign affairs. As a consequence, the solutions of today's problems require joint legislative-executive cooperation on a scale heretofore unknown in American history. . . .
>
> The Constitution is not at all precise in its allocation of foreign affairs powers between the two branches.
>
> Given the present constitutional framework and the attitude of the legislative branch toward foreign affairs, the situation calls for mutual cooperation and restraint. The executive branch must appreciate the role of the Congress and the propriety of its participation in foreign affairs

where legislative decisions are required. Similarly, the Congress should appreciate that leadership in the conduct of foreign affairs can come only from the executive side of the Government and that the Congress should not attempt to participate in executive decisions in the international field.

Today's global diplomacy makes joint executive-legislative policy-making a necessity in several fields: climate, energy, and humanitarian interventions, among them.

IMPLICATIONS FOR THE DEPARTMENT OF STATE

What do the current and likely future challenges to the well-being of the United States mean for the State Department? These challenges call for a greater emphasis on policy planning and the conduct of diplomacy in the following areas:

1. Managing challenges posed by the arrival of the leading edge of a new global system.

2. Creating global and regional regimes necessary to deal with a set of existential threats to humanity.

3. Responding to broad threats to the states system derived from traditional challenges, such as a desire to erase borders or enlarge the scope of religious or secular ideologies in the governance of states and eventually the system as a whole.

This introduction of new priorities or a re-ordering of priorities does not require a wholesale reorganization of the State Department. Most of the traditional business of the State Department should proceed with little change, except for a heightened awareness on the part of policymakers and those who practice diplomacy of the broader context in which they are operating.

Relations between the major world powers will still require

careful tending. Security threats arising from military programs or operations will have to be confronted. Economic interests will require support. The human dimension will remain an important factor determining the quality of the relationship. But changes are required in the American agenda with other major powers. The emphasis should be on:

- More conversations about ground rules as features of a new global system become more apparent.
- Creation of a set of new or revised global commons.
- Adjustments in the way the states system has worked to confront, for example, new modes of power-sharing between national governments and private groups and threats to diversity posed by the introduction of violent private groups with doctrinaire ideologies into the international system of states.

THE PRACTICE OF DIPLOMACY

Crisis management, another form of diplomacy frequently practiced by the State Department, will remain necessary with large and small states alike. Two other forms of policymaking and diplomacy will have to be elevated significantly in the State Department: "preventive" and "order-building" diplomacy.[5]

Preventive diplomacy is defined by the United Nations as: "Diplomatic action to prevent disputes from arising between parties, to prevent existing disputes from escalating into conflict and to limit the spread of conflicts when they occur."[6]

Order-building diplomacy means the step-by-step creation of norms, rules, and institutions among states, aimed at building a lasting order based on common values. Joining with other nations in pursuit of some common goal is perhaps the most familiar example of the building-block approach to creating a stable international order.

In a time of transition and uncertainty, American diplomacy

must improve its capacity to head off conflicts while building the framework for global order. These are not tasks that should be bundled into a new bureau or special office. Each geographic bureau in the State Department has the capacity to identify and foresee the likely course of conflicts. Solutions to existential threats to humanity and ideas about adapting to the new characteristics of global relations are readily available in many corners of the department. What seems to be missing is a mechanism for senior officials to deal with the important, instead of the merely urgent. This is probably more a matter of mindset than of organization.

This kind of exploration of mega-trends and the American response to them is conducted effectively by the National Intelligence Council (NIC) and by private groups like the International Crisis Group. Institutionalized meetings of senior State Department officials with the NIC or, on occasion, with private organizations would strengthen the State Department's capacity for preventive and order-building diplomacy.

STAFFING THE STATE DEPARTMENT

The Foreign Service of the United States is supposed to be a corps of professional diplomats capable of carrying out the nation's foreign policies both at home and abroad. The civil service provides a permanent staff for the State Department which allows it to be the repository of a depth of expertise in certain areas that Foreign Service officers sacrifice by their frequent rotation from post to post. In an important study released on April 1, 2015, entitled "American Diplomacy at Risk," several senior American retired diplomats presented their findings regarding the profession of diplomacy in the United States.[7] The report persuasively argues that the intention of the Foreign Service Act of 1980 to create a professional corps of top-notch diplomats has been undermined by a failure to encourage this goal in practice. This has led to the de-professionalization of America's diplomatic corps. The report contains several recommendations regarding the relationships between the Foreign Service and the civil service which deserve careful attention and action by this and future administrations.

One of the most important issues relates to current personnel policy. Writing in the *Foreign Service Journal* of January/February 2016, Ambassador Thomas Boyatt spelled out the differences in personnel practices between the early 1980s and the present time:

> Then, only one of the regional assistant secretaries was a political appointee and all deputies were career officers. Ninety-nine percent of the officer-level positions in the regional bureaus were FSOs, as were more than fifty percent of the functional bureau positions. There were perhaps two special representatives or ambassadors at large.
>
> Today, political appointees at the assistant secretary level and above outnumber career officers, and political deputy assistant secretaries approach thirty percent.

Obviously, the goal of endowing the nation with a top-notch corps of professional diplomats is not possible to achieve under these circumstances. Future administrations will have to reverse these personnel policies or accept a second-rate diplomatic establishment that will not match the diplomatic corps of other advanced nations such as the United Kingdom.

The first approach to policy formation has to be diagnosing a problem properly so that policymakers are addressing real issues rather than fanciful ones. The late Stanford professor Alexander George identified this deficit in American foreign policy machinery over twenty years ago, but the deficit remains with us today.[8] He wrote that "in thinking about the kind of policy-relevant knowledge that needs to be developed we should give more attention to its contribution to the diagnosis of problem situations than to its ability to prescribe sound choices of policy." What he was talking about can be summed up in his remark about President Kennedy's handling of the Cuban Missile Crisis: "As Llewellyn Thompson's contribution during the Cuban missile crisis indicates, area experts and diplomats have a particularly critical contribution to make to the development of sophisticated images of adversaries."

Of course, area expertise can be acquired through many years of overseas postings. In years past, it could be acquired through studies at universities. That source of knowledge of foreign societies and their leadership is less available now. The problem is described in an article written by Charles King in a recent edition of *Foreign Affairs*.[9] As he puts it:

Educational institutions and the disciplines they preserve are retreating from the task of cultivating men and women who are comfortable moving around the globe, both literally and figuratively. Government agencies, in turn, are reducing their overall support and narrowing to fields deemed relevant to U.S. national security—and even to specific research topics within them.[10]

THE EDUCATION OF DIPLOMATS

The situation cries out for some method of building area expertise within the Department of State. For the first time in its history, the British Foreign and Commonwealth Office has established a diplomatic academy. The British foreign minister at the time of the announcement, William Hague, told the House of Commons that his vision was:

. . . a Foreign Office that is an international center of ideas and expertise; that leads foreign policy thinking across government; that is recognized as the best diplomatic service in the world; and that is able to defend our country's interests in an unpredictable and competitive international landscape for the long term.[11]

That statement could also become the goal for the George P. Shultz National Foreign Affairs Training Center (NFATC). The director of the British diplomatic academy, Jon Davies, visited the center in November 2014. He later remarked that the British had drawn heavily on the experiences of the center and envied the resources secured for it.[12]

In the introduction to "American Diplomacy at Risk," the authors raise some fundamental criticisms about today's Department of State:

- American diplomacy is increasingly politicized, reversing a century-long effort to create a merit-based system of high professionalism.

- The State Department and the Foreign Service have weakened the capacity for diplomacy by failing to pay sufficient attention to professional education and assignments that develop America's future leaders.

Recommendation 19 of the report envisages "the establishment of the National Diplomatic University at the National Foreign Affairs Training Center." Explaining the purpose of this, the authors of the report simply said it "would manage and deliver the professional education needed to prepare FSOs and staff to meet the challenges of 21st century diplomacy."

Thomas A. Shannon Jr., under secretary for political affairs, has urged that scholars and diplomats cultivate a close working relationship.[13] The basic purpose would be "to create a public policy intellectual setting where we can benefit mutually from our work. We need to create a setting where we can build a narrative and purpose to describe and inform our long diplomacy."

Ambassador Shannon points out that in academia there has been "a decline in the ability to analyze and synthesize information across disciplines and then to build a narrative that explains political, economic, and social phenomena."

He obviously hopes that this deficiency can be overcome through the process of systematically organizing studies involving scholars and diplomats. To launch a program like this he suggests a gathering convened by the secretary of state "to bring together presidents of leading universities, respected academics, and influential opinion makers to set an agenda for cooperation and create the mechanisms necessary to promote collaborations."

This idea certainly deserves serious consideration, yet I wonder whether the gap between scholar and diplomat can be bridged in this fashion. I suspect that an institution will have to be created that becomes a model for the kind of policy analysis that Shannon rightly says is so badly needed in a time of transition.

Charles A. Ray, a retired FSO, has written a thoughtful article in the same issue of *The Foreign Service Journal* in which the establishment of a British diplomatic academy was reported. One of Ray's conclusions was that "a system of professional education" should be established for the Foreign Service. He suggested that it could be either at the Foreign Service Institute or through a cooperative agreement with universities in the Washington area.

My own conclusion is that the NFATC should become the core of what Ray calls "a system of professional education." It is not that now. As Ray observes, "We in the Foreign Service are lucky to get much beyond language and tradecraft training."

The next administration should make it a priority to raise the stature of the NFATC in area studies to the equivalent of a first-class American university. In a 2014 report of a group set up by the American Foreign Service Association, a recommendation was offered that the Foreign Service Institute should become an accredited degree-granting institution as soon as practicable, citing master's degrees as the place to begin, possibly in collaboration with universities. This goal should certainly be endorsed by a future administration as an early step in reinventing the Shultz National Foreign Affairs Training Center.

CLOSING NOTE

THE ART AND PRACTICE OF GOVERNANCE

George P. Shultz

arlier I remarked on the importance of being a "good gardener" in managing foreign affairs. But the analogy holds in our domestic processes too. Two things stand out as I survey the ideas within this American "blueprint" against the longer arc of our country's history.

First, it is tempting to think that the problems we face today are somehow of a different nature than the ones that came before. But for all the day-to-day noise in Washington, our government's most important priorities remain much the same as ever:

- Managing our spending so as to achieve public aims without putting a drag on the wider economy.

- Usefully guiding private enterprise through regulation that does not snuff out its spark.

- Responsibly handling the monetary lever across economic cycles.

- Confronting the trade-offs in the affordability of our social safety net.

- Asserting our country's global alliances and security objectives.

- Educating the next generation and dealing with the fact that the United States continues to be the most desirable place in the world to make home.

All would be familiar to the founding fathers. And none are directly soluble problems. We cannot declare victory through one Congress, or one president, or one treaty; instead, they must be continually worked at.

This leads me to the second observation, which was also remarked on by many of our *Blueprint* authors: our government continues to suffer from a lack of long-term thinking. It is hard to keep working at our most important priorities in a sincere way if we do not have a basic vision to support that. Our energies and attention get drawn up into the next crisis served up atop the political agenda. Instead, the political environment should make room for competent individuals to work in good faith toward matters that will be good for the country, even if they do not offer immediate rewards.

Common to both these observations is the role of good governance. Governance is a process, not an end in itself. But none of the policy goals in this "blueprint" can be sustained without it. In that spirit, I'd like to conclude our efforts here with some simple observations from my own experience on things that could help.

THE ROLE OF TRUST IN GOVERNANCE

Right now, our country faces a crisis of competence in area after area. We see a government that does not seem to work well. An essential element in government, and in any good negotiation, is trust. You need to be confident that your counterpart will deliver on promises made.

Campaigning is an act of division—the exact opposite of governance, which is an act of inclusion and the finding of common ground. Our political system right now has too much campaigning, and that complicates governance and the establishment of trust.

So, for governance to have the high quality we need, we must remember that trust is the coin of the realm.

THE ROLE OF INDIVIDUAL COMPETENCY
AND RESPONSIBILITY IN GOVERNANCE

More prosaically, the operation of government can also be sharply improved if more A-list players are brought into government service, arranging the structure of government so that they have real responsibility. Right now, a trend that has been in evidence for some time has reached an extreme. The White House and the people working there with the president (including the now much-too-large staff of the National Security Council) dominate policymaking and, more and more, the execution of policy.

At the same time, someone who is nominated to a presidential post faces a grueling prospect. First, there is a lengthy questionnaire that must be filled out, requiring the employment of a lawyer and an accountant. Then the nomination is forwarded to the Senate, which takes its time. At the end of December 2014, there were 133 people who had been nominated and reported out favorably by their Senate committees, but they had yet to receive a confirmation vote in the Senate. They were kept in limbo, awaiting re-nomination in the new Congress. That is an unattractive prospect for anyone, especially A-list players. And when they are finally in office, they find the White House-centric process of governance means that their capacities are not fully used. So, many alpha players who would normally be ready to serve simply bail out.

This could be easily remedied if the president announced that he will govern through the people who are nominated and confirmed in their positions. The nomination process can be changed dramatically. Do an FBI and IRS check, followed by the statement, "If you have skeletons in your closet, don't come." The president will announce that cabinet officers will be regarded as his staff for developing policy in various areas. These are also constitutionally accountable people who, unlike White House aides, can be called to testify at any time. This will give the policymaking process access to career people who have lots of experience and can contribute in important ways to the development of policies. Also, in the end, these are the people who will take a big part in the execution of policy.

With this approach, the president can go to the Senate and say, "I expect a prompt up-or-down vote on my nominees, and I expect them to be given the benefit of the doubt since these are people with whom I have chosen to work."

BUDGETING AS A STRUCTURAL FRAMEWORK

Congress also needs to continue to shape up. The Constitution gives the legislative branch the power of the purse. Let's stay on track the old-fashioned way where hearings are held with subunits of each department and a budget is developed from the bottom up. This requires members of Congress to work hard, so they can know well the units of government whose funding they oversee. Earlier votes on gigantic sums of money and continuing resolutions are a cop-out by Congress. They mean that Congress has not responsibly carried out the power of the purse given to it by the Constitution.

In 2012 and 2014, the Senate failed to approve any one of the twelve appropriations bills. In 2015, at last, the House and Senate agreed to a budget resolution; the House Appropriations Committee reported out nine of twelve appropriations bills and the full House approved six of them. Similarly on schedule, the Senate Appropriations Committee reported out five bills.

If these changes are made, the quality of policy and execution will improve. The revised processes will put more emphasis on the very large nonpartisan element in the process of governance, so the atmosphere will change for the better.

GOVERNING OVER DIVERSITY IN AN AGE OF TRANSPARENCY

Such changes are essential now since the very process of governance is changing rapidly and the developments bringing this about will only intensify as time goes by. The availability of information and the ability of people to communicate with each other, including across international boundaries, seem limitless. People everywhere, with only minimum effort, can find out almost anything. Cell phones are widespread and widely used, so people can communicate with each other and organize. Their diverse interests must somehow be dealt with. All of this is relatively new. But for governance in this age to come to be successful, these developments need to be recognized since they are permanent and will not disappear.

Diversity expresses itself in many ways: religion, ethnicity, color, and economic well-being. Diversity has always existed, and has had an impact on governance; and while some have recognized diversity, it has also been possible to ignore or suppress it. No more. Taken as a whole, new information and communication technologies enhance the freedom of individuals to think for themselves, to believe whatever they believe, and to question whatever is taking place. A new freedom emerges to question and even to replace ruling authorities. The ability to challenge authority, even legitimate authority, can easily extend to actions that may be good for the populace as a whole but less beneficial for part of it. That part now demands to be heard.

From the standpoint of anyone charged with the responsibility of governance, the fragmentation and the power of dissident groups can easily swamp the coherence needed for effective governance. We as a country have faced similar problems in earlier times and have prevailed.

Despite real tensions—which could also be resolved by better governance—we have the most successful diverse culture and population of any major economy. Indeed, we should work on making this more of a comparative advantage in a fiercely competitive global economy. And we have a military of remarkable diversity and capability too, which will remain so for as long as support is strong and enduring and its objectives are clear and manageable.

These advantages are not immutable, and in recent years nothing has worked so effectively to our disadvantage as the irresponsibility and short-sightedness of many in the American political class. Yet we remain optimistic.

We can make progress on all of the issues that trouble us. With sensible policies—such as those outlined in this *Blueprint*—combined with a renewed effort to restore to America the highest standards of governance, we can renew our nation's economic strength and provide broadly rising standards of living to all our citizens. President Reagan often said, "Democracy is not a spectator sport." We all need to join the effort to restore America to its optimal strength. Our economic well-being and that of our children is at stake. So, too, is America's global influence and, with it, the security and well-being of vast swaths of the world, whose people rely upon us to promote peace and progress for all.

NOTES / REFERENCES

CHAPTER 4: TRANSFORMATIONAL HEALTH CARE REFORM

1. For instance, Robinson and Miller reported (J.C. Robinson and K. Miller; Total Expenditures per Patient in Hospital-Owned and Physician-Owned Physician Organizations in California; JAMA. 2014; 312(16): 1663–1669. doi:10.1001/jama.2014.14072) that when hospitals owned doctor groups, per patient expenditures increased 10–20%, or up to $1,700 extra per patient per year. Capps (C. Capps, D. Dranove, C. Ody; "The Effect of Hospital Acquisitions of Physician Practices on Prices and Spending"; Institute for Policy Research, Northwestern University, Working Paper Series, February 2015) found that specialist services prices increased by 34% after joining a health system.

2. Sean P. Keehan, Gigi A. Cuckler, Andrea M. Sisko, Andrew J. Madison, Sheila D. Smith, Devin A. Stone, John A. Poisal, Christian J. Wolfe, and Joseph M. Lizonitz, "National health expenditure projections, 2014–2024: Spending growth faster than recent trends," *Health Affairs* 34 (2015): 1407-1417, http://content.healthaffairs.org/content/early/2015/07/15/hlthaff .2015.0600.

3. Centers for Medicare and Medicaid Services, "Medicaid & CHIP: February 2015 Monthly Applications, Eligibility Determinations and Enrollment Report," May 2015.

4. Report to the Congress: Medicare and the Health Care Delivery System, MedPac, June 2015.

5. National Research Council and National Academy of Public Administration, "Choosing the Nation's Fiscal Future" (Washington, DC: National Academies Press, 2010).

6. See, for example, Soeren Mattke, Edward Kelley, Peter Scherer, Jeremy Hurst, Maria Luisa Gil Lapetra, and the HCQI Expert Group Members, "Health Care Quality Indicators Project: Initial Indicators Report,"

OECD Health Working Papers no. 22 (2006); Sandra Garcia Armesto, Maria Luisa Gil Lapetra, Lihan Wei, Edward Kelley, and the Members of the HCQI Expert Group, "Health Care Quality Indicators Project 2006: Data Collection Update Report," OECD Working Papers, no. 29 (2007); M.J. Quinn, "Cancer Trends in the United States—A View From Europe," *Journal of the National Cancer Institute* 95, no. 17 (2003): 1258–1261; Gemma Gatta, Riccardo Capocaccia, Michel P. Coleman, Lynn A. Gloeckler Ries, Timo Hakulinen, Andrea Micheli, Milena Sant, Arduino Verdecchia, and Franco Berrino, "Toward a Comparison of Survival in American and European Cancer Patients," *Cancer* 89, no. 4 (August 2000): 899; Laura Ciccolallo, Riccardo Capocaccia, Michel P. Coleman, Franco Berrino, J.S. Coebergh, R.A. Damhuis, J. Faivre, C. Martinez-Garcia, H. Møller, M. Ponz de Leon, G. Launoy, N. Raverdy, E. M. Williams, and Gemma Gatta, "Survival Differences Between European and US Patients with Colorectal Cancer: Role of Stage at Diagnosis and Surgery," *Gut* 54, no. 2 (2005): 268–273; David H. Howard, Lisa C. Richardson, and Kenneth E. Thorpe, "Cancer Screening And Age in The United States And Europe," *Health Affairs* 28, no. 6 (2009): 1838–47; June O'Neill and Dave M. O'Neill, "Health Status, Health Care and Inequality: Canada vs. the U.S.," National Bureau of Economic Research, NBER Working Paper 13429 (September 2007); Mike Richards, "The size of the prize for earlier diagnosis of cancer in England," *British Journal of Cancer* 101, suppl. 2 (December 3, 2009): S125–9; Eija-Riitta Salomaa, Susanna Sällinen, Heikki Hiekkanen, and Kari Liippo, "Delays in the Diagnosis and Treatment of Lung Cancer," *Chest* 128 (2005): 2282–2288; Eilish O'Regan, "Public patients face up to five-year wait to see a specialist," *The Independent*, March 25, 2011, http://www.inde pendent.ie/health/latest-news/public-patients-face-up-to-fiveyear-wait-to -see-a-specialist-2594298.html; Jeremy Hurst and Luigi Siciliani, "Tackling Excessive Waiting Times for Elective Surgery: A Comparison of Policies in Twelve OECD Countries," annexes 1,2,3, OECD Health Working Papers, no. 6 (2003); Bacchus Barua and Frazier Fathers, "Waiting your turn: Wait times for health care in Canada, 2014 Report," Fraser Institute, November 26, 2014; Merritt Hawkins, "Physician Appointment Wait Times and Medicaid and Medicare Acceptance Rates," 2014 Survey; Cathy Schoen, Robin Osborn, David Squires, Michelle M. Doty, Roz Pierson, and Sandra Applebaum, "The Commonwealth Fund 2010 International Health Policy Survey in Eleven Countries," The Commonwealth Fund, November 2010; Katharina Wolf-Maier, Richard S. Cooper, Holly Kramer, José R. Banegas, Simona Giampaoli, Michel R. Joffres, Neil Poulter, Paola Primatesta, Birgitta Stegmayr, and Michael Thamm, "Hypertension Treatment and Control in Five European Countries, Canada, and the United States," *Hypertension* 43, no. 1 (January 2004): 10–17; Kenneth E. Thorpe, David

H. Howard, and Katya Galactionova, "Differences In Disease Prevalence As a Source of the U.S.-European Health Care Spending Gap," *Health Affairs* 26, no. 6 (October 2007): 678–686; Eileen M. Crimmins, Krista Garcia, and Jung Ki Kim, "Are International Differences in Health Similar to International Differences in Life Expectancy?" National Research Council (Washington, DC: National Academies Press, 2010); Eileen M. Crimmins, Samuel H. Preston, and Barney Cohen, eds., "International Differences in Mortality at Older Ages: Dimensions and Sources," Panel on Understanding Divergent Trends in Longevity in High-Income Countries, Committee on Population, Division of Behavioral and Social Sciences and Education (Washington, DC: National Academies Press, 2010); tables 3.4 and 3.6; June E. O'Neill and Dave M. O'Neill, "Health Status, Health Care and Inequality: Canada vs. the U.S.," NBER Working Paper no. 13429 (September 2007); Bacchus Barua, Nadeem Esmail, and Taylor Jackson, "The Effect of Wait Times on Mortality in Canada," Fraser Institute, May 2014; Matthew G. Snider, Steven J. MacDonald, and Ralph Pototschnik," Waiting times and patient perspectives for total hip and knee arthroplasty in rural and urban Ontario," *Canadian Journal of Surgery* 48, no. 5 (2005): 355–360; Jean Ethier, David C. Mendelssohn, Stacey J. Elder, Takeshi Hasegawa, Tadao Akizawa, Takashi Akiba, Bernard J. Canaud, and Ronald L. Pisoni, "Vascular access use and outcomes: an international perspective from the dialysis outcomes and practice patterns study," *Nephrology Dialysis Transplantation* 23 (2008): 3219–3226; Lynelle Moon, Pierre Moise, Stephane Jacobzone, and the ARD-Stroke Experts Group, "Stroke care in OECD countries: a comparison of treatment, costs, and outcomes in 17 countries," OECD Health Working Papers, no. 5 (June 2003), table A2.6; Robert J. Blendon, Cathy Schoen, Catherine M. DesRoches, Robin Osborn, Kinga Zapert, and Elizabeth Raleigh, "Confronting Competing Demands To Improve Quality: A Five-Country Hospital Survey," *Health Affairs* 23, no. 3 (May 2004): 119–135; Agency for Healthcare Research and Quality, "Technology Assessment: Cardiac Catheterization in Freestanding Clinics," September 7, 2005; John Z. Ayanian and Thomas J. Quinn, "Quality Of Care For Coronary Heart Disease In Two Countries," *Health Affairs* 20, no. 3 (May 2001): 55–67; Mark O. Baerlocher, "Canada's slow adoption of new technologies adds burden to health care system," *Canadian Medical Association Journal* 176, no. 5 (February 2007): 616; European Federation of Pharmaceutical Industries and Associations, "The Pharmaceutical Industry in Figures," 2011; Bengt Jonsson and Nils Wilking, "Market uptake of new oncology drugs," *Annals of Oncology* 18, supplement 3 (2007): iii31–iii48, doi:10.1093/annonc/mdm099; Peter Mitchell, "Price controls seen as key to Europe's drug innovation lag," *Nature Reviews Drug Discovery* 6 (April 2007): 257–258, doi:10.1038/nrd2293; Tufts Center for the Study of Drug

Development, "While total approvals decline, U.S. is preferred market for first launch," *Impact Report* 10, no. 6 (November/December 2008); Scott W. Atlas, "Evaluating Access to America's Medical Care," in *In Excellent Health: Setting the Record Straight on America's Health Care* (Stanford, CA: Hoover Institution Press, 2011), 159–210.

7. Scott W. Atlas, "Measuring Medical Care Quality in the United States," in *In Excellent Health,* 97–158; Arduino Verdecchia, Silvia Francisci, Hermann Brenner, Gemma Gatta, Andrea Micheli, Lucia Mangone, Ian Kunkler, and the EUROCARE-4 Working Group, "Recent cancer survival in Europe: a 2000–02 period analysis of EUROCARE-4 data," *Lancet Oncology* 8, no. 9 (September 2007): 784–796; F. Levi, F. Lucchini, E. Negri, and C. La Vecchia, "Trends in mortality from cardiovascular and cerebrovascular diseases in Europe and other areas of the world," *Heart* 88 (2002): 119–124; P. Kaul, P. Armstrong, W. Chang, C. Naylor, C. Granger, K. Lee, I. Peterson, R. Califf, E. Topol, and D. Mark, 2004, "Long-term Mortality of Patients with Acute Myocardial Infarction in the United States and Canada," *Circulation* 110 (2004): 1754–60; Melissa L. Martinson, Julien O. Teitler, and Nancy E. Reichman, "Health Across the Lifespan in the United States and England," *American Journal of Epidemiology* 173, no. 8 (2011); Ayanian and Quinn, "Quality of care for coronary heart disease in two countries"; H.C. Wijeysundera, M. Machado, F. Farahati, X. Wang, W. Witteman, G. van der Velde, J.V. Tu, D.W. Lee, S.G. Goodman, R. Petrella, M. O'Flaherty, M. Krahn, and S. Capewell, "Association of temporal trends in risk factors and treatment uptake with coronary heart disease mortality, 1994–2005," Journal of the American Medical Association 303 (2010): 1841–1847; Thorpe, Howard, and Galactionova, "Differences In Disease Prevalence"; Wolf-Maier et al., "Hypertension Treatment and Control"; Y.R. Wang, G.C. Alexander, and R.S. Stafford, "Outpatient hypertension treatment, treatment intensification, and control in Western Europe and the United States," *Archives of Internal Medicine* 167 (2007): 141–147; E. Gakidou, L. Mallinger, J. Abbott-Klafter, R. Guerrero, S. Villalpando, R.L. Ridaura, W. Aekplakorn, M. Naghavi, S. Lim, R. Lozano, and C.J. Murray, "Management of diabetes and associated cardiovascular risk factors in seven countries: a comparison of data from national health examination surveys," *Bulletin of the World Health Organization* 89 (2011): 172–183.

8. See for example Almeida C, Braveman P, Gold MR, Szwarcwald CL, Ribeiro JM, Miglionico A, Millar JS, Porto S, Costa NR, Rubio VO, Segall M, Starfield B, Travassos C, Uga A, Valente J, Viacava F., "Methodological concerns and recommendations on policy consequences of the World Health Report 2000," *Lancet* 357 (2001): 1692; P. Musgrove, "Judging health systems: reflections on WHO's methods," *Lancet* 361 (2003): 1817–1820;

E. Ollila and M. Koivusalo, "The World Health Report 2000: The World Health Organization health policy steering off-course—changed values, poor evidence, and lack of accountability," *International Journal of Health Services* 32 (2002): 503–514; Scott W. Atlas, "The WHO Ranking of Health Systems Redux: A Critical Appraisal," in *In Excellent Health*, 1–18.

9. Federal Subsidies for Health Insurance Coverage for People Under Age 65: 2016 to 2026, March 24, 2016; Congressional Budget Office.

10. Q3 2014 Health Insurance Enrollment: Employer Coverage Continues to Decline, Medicaid Keeps Growing; E.F. Haislmaier and D. Gonshorowski, Heritage Foundation BACKGROUNDER No. 2988, January 29, 2015 (http://www.heritage.org/research/reports/2015/01/q3-2014-health-insurance-enrollment-employer-coverage-continues-to-decline-medicaid-keeps-growing).

11. Centers for Medicare and Medicaid Services, "National Health Expenditure Projections 2012-2022."

12. HSC Health Tracking Physician Survey, 2008.

13. Merritt Hawkins, "Physician Appointment Wait Times."

14. Department of Health and Human Services, "Access to Care: Provider Availability in Medicaid Managed Care," December 2014.

15. Merritt Hawkins, "2014 Survey of America's Physicians," Merritt Hawkins for the Physicians' Foundation.

16. Merritt Hawkins, "A Survey of America's Physicians: Practice Patterns and Perspectives," The Physicians' Foundation survey by Merritt Hawkins, September 2012.

17. See for example: Michael A. Gaglia, "Effect of Insurance Type on Adverse Cardiac Events after Percutaneous Coronary Intervention," *American Journal of Cardiology* 107 (2011): 675–80; D. J. LaPar et al., "Primary Payer Status Affects Mortality for Major Surgical Operations," Annals of Surgery 252 (2010): 544–51; J. Kwok et al., "The Impact of Health Insurance Status on the Survival of Patients with Head and Neck Cancer," *Cancer* 116 (2010): 476–85; R. R. Kelz et al., "Morbidity and Mortality of Colorectal Carcinoma Differs by Insurance Status," *Cancer* 101 (2004): 2187–94; J. G. Allen et al., "Insurance Status Is an Independent Predictor of Long-Term Survival after Lung Transplantation in the United States," *Journal of Heart and Lung Transplantation* 30 (2011): 45–53.

18. Insurance Coverage Provisions of the Affordable Care Act— CBO's January 2015, Congressional Budget Office.

19. Avalere Health, "Trendwatch Chartbook 2014: Trends affecting hospitals and health systems," prepared for the American Hospital Association, 2014.

20. A. Senger, "Measuring Choice and Competition in the Exchanges:

Still Worse than Before the ACA," Heritage Foundation, Issue Brief 4324 on Health Care, December 22, 2014.

21. McKinsey Center for U.S. Health System Reform, "Hospital networks: Configurations on the exchanges and their impact on premiums," 2013 and 2015.

22. Avalere Health, "Exchange Plans Include 34 Percent Fewer Providers than the Average for Commercial Plans," June 2015.

23. Avalere Health, "Access to Comprehensive Stroke Centers & Specialty Physicians in Exchange Plans," prepared for the American Heart Association, September 2014.

24. Kaiser Family Foundation, "Employee Health Benefits Annual Surveys, 2007-2014," http://kff.org/health-costs/report/employer-health-bene fits-annual-survey-archives.

25. Amelia M. Haviland, Matthew D. Eisenberg, Ateev Mehrotra, Peter J. Huckfeldt, Neeraj Sood "Do 'Consumer-Directed' Health Plans Bend the Cost Curve Over Time?" NBER Working Paper no. 21031, March 2015, http://www.nber.org/papers/w21031.

26. Amelia M. Haviland, Neeraj Sood, Roland McDevitt, and M. Susan Marquis, "How Do Consumer Directed Health Plans Affect Vulnerable Populations?" *Forum for Health Economics and Policy* 14, no. 2 (2011): 1558-9544.

27. Amelia M. Haviland, Neeraj Sood, Roland D. McDevitt, and M. Susan Marquis, "The effects of consumer-directed health plans on episodes of health care," *Forum for Health Economics and Policy* 14, no. 2 (2011):1–27, http://www.rand.org/pubs/external_publications/EP201100208.html.

28. S-J. Wu, G. Sylwestrzak, C. Shah, and A. DeVries, "Price transparency for MRIs increased use of less costly providers and triggered provider competition," *Health Affairs* 33 (2014): 1391-1398, http://content.health affairs.org/content/33/8/1391.abstract.

29. J.C. Robinson, T. Brown, and C. Whaley, "Reference-Based Benefit Design Changes Consumers' Choices And Employers' Payments For Ambulatory Surgery," *Health Affairs* 34 (2015): 415–422, http://content .healthaffairs.org/content/34/3/415.abstract.

30. Scott W. Atlas, analysis of "EHB Annual Survey Data, 2006–2014," Kaiser Family Foundation.

31. Edmund F. Haislmaier and Drew Gonshorowski, "Responding to King v. Burwell: Congress's first step should be to remove costly mandates driving up premiums," Heritage Foundation, Issue Brief no. 4400, May 2015.

32. Health Insurance Mandates in the States, 2012; Victoria Craig Bunce; Council for Affordable Health Insurance 2013.

33. Comprehensive assessment of ACA factors that will affect individual market premiums in 2014, J.T. O'Connor; Milliman (https://www.ahip.org /MillimanReportACA04252013/).

34. American Academy of Actuaries, "Issue Brief: Drivers of 2016 Health Insurance Premium Changes," August 2015.

35. J. Schroeder, Doermer School of Business and Management Sciences, Indiana University–Purdue University Fort Wayne, 2007.

36. B.E. Garrett, S.R. Dube, A. Trosclair, R.S. Caraballo, T.F. Pechacek; Centers for Disease Control and Prevention (CDC), "Cigarette Smoking: United States, 1965–2008," Morbidity and Mortality Weekly Report, Centers for Disease Control and Prevention, Supplements, January 14, 2011.

37. E.A. Finkelstein, O.A. Khavjou, H. Thompson, J.G. Trogdon, L. Pan, B. Sherry, W. Dietz, "Obesity and Severe Obesity Forecasts Through 2030," *American Journal of Preventive Medicine* 42, no. 6 (2012): 563–570.

38. D. Withrow and D.A. Alter, "The economic burden of obesity worldwide: a systematic review of the direct costs of obesity," *Obesity Reviews* 12 (2011): 131–141.

39. R.A. Hammond and R. Levine, "The economic impact of obesity in the United States," *Diabetes, Metabolic Syndrome and Obesity: Targets and Therapy* 3 (2010): 285–295.

40. Devenir Research, "2015 Midyear HSA Market Statistics & Trends," August 11, 2015.

41. A. Haviland, M.S. Marquis, R.D. McDevitt, and N. Sood, "Growth of Consumer Directed Health Plans to One-Half of All Employer-Sponsored Insurance Could Save $57 billion Annually," *Health Affairs* 31, no. 5 (2012): 1009–15, http://content.healthaffairs.org/content/31/5/1009.full.

42. L.L. Berry, A.M. Mirabito, and W.B. Baun, "What's the Hard Return on Employee Wellness Programs?" *Harvard Business Review*, December 2010.

43. Jonathan Gruber, "The Tax Exclusion for Employer-Sponsored Health Insurance," *National Tax Journal* 62, no. 2, part 2 (June 2011): 511–530.

44. Congressional Budget Office, "Options for Reducing the Deficit: 2014 to 2023," November 2013, see health revenues, option 15, page 243 2, http://www.cbo.gov/sites/default/files/cbofiles/attachments/44715-Options ForReducingDeficit-3.pdf.

45. S. Lowry, "Itemized Tax Deductions for Individuals: Data Analysis," Congressional Research Service, February 2014, https://www.fas.org /sgp/crs/misc/R43012.pdf.

46. For example, A. Finkelstein, "The Aggregate Effects of Health Insurance: Evidence from the Introduction of Medicare," *Quarterly Journal of Economics* 122 (2007): 1–37.

47. J.M. Ortman, V.A. Velkoff, and H. Hogan, "An Aging Nation: The Older Population in the United States: Population Estimates and Projection," Current Population Reports, May 2014: P25–1140.

48. AMA National Health Insurer Report Card 2013, American Medical Association, 2013 (https://www.trizetto.com/WorkArea/DownloadAsset .aspx?id=6385).

49. Merritt Hawkins, "2014 Survey of America's Physicians," Merritt Hawkins for the Physicians' Foundation.

50. S.P. Keehan, G.A. Cuckler, A.M. Sisko, A.J. Madison, S.D. Smith, D.A. Stone, J.A. Poisal, C.J. Wolfe, J.M. Lizonitz, "National health expenditure projections, 2014–2024: Spending growth faster than recent trends," *Health Affairs* 34 (2015): 1407-1417, http://content.healthaffairs.org/con tent/early/2015/07/15/hlthaff.2015.0600.

51. "Questions about the ACA Medicaid expansion," Alison Mitchell; Memorandum, Congressional Research Service, January 30, 2015.

52. A. Mehrotra, H. Liu, J.L. Adams, M.C. Wang, J.R. Lave, N.M. Thygeson, L.I. Solberg, E.A. McGlynn, "Comparing costs and quality of care at retail clinics with that of other medical settings for 3 common illnesses," *Annals of Internal Medicine* 151, (2009): 321–328.

53. Accenture, "Retail Medical Clinics: From Foe to Friend?" June 2013.

54. Institute of Medicine, "The Future of Nursing: Leading Change, Advancing Health" (Washington, DC: National Academies Press, 2011), http://www.nap.edu/catalog/12956/the-future-of-nursing-leading-change -advancing-health.

55. The Complexities of Physician Supply and Demand: Projections Through 2025; Michael J. Dill and Edward S. Salsberg, Center for Workforce Studies, Association of American Medical Colleges,

56. 2014 Global R&D Funding Forecast, Battelle, R&D Magazine, December 2013.

57. J. Makower, A. Meer, and L. Denend, "FDA Impact on US Medical Technology Innovation: A Survey of Over 200 Medical Technology Companies," November 2010.

58. Vivek Wadhwa, "The Immigrant Exodus: Why America Is Losing the Global Race to Capture Entrepreneurial Talent," Wharton Digital Press, Philadelphia 2012.

59. Scott W. Atlas, "The Surprising International Consensus on Healthcare," *Defining Ideas*, June 19, 2014; Scott W. Atlas, ed., *Reforming America's Health Care System: The Flawed Vision of ObamaCare* (Stanford, CA: Hoover Institution Press, 2010); Atlas, *In Excellent Health.*

60. CEA Insurers of Europe, "Private medical insurance in the European Union," 2011.

61. For example: In the United Kingdom alone, the total number of

patients on the waiting list for diagnosis or start of treatment reached 3.4 million in May 2015, the highest since 2008, including the 11.8 percent of hospitalized patients whose wait exceeded eighteen weeks; 18 percent of UK cancer patients referred for "urgent treatment" were forced to wait more than two full months for initiation of treatment (see www.england.nhs.uk; NHS Quarterly Monitoring Report, July, 2015, Kings Fund).

62. NHS 2014 budget, The NHS budget and how it has changed, The King's Fund.

63. LaingBuisson Consultancy, "Health Cover: UK Market Report," 12th ed., 2015.

64. Svensk Forsakring, "Insurance in Sweden: Statistics 2013."

65. June, 2015 survey; Rasmussen Reports.

66. April, 2015 survey; Rasmussen Reports.

CHAPTER 6: NATIONAL AND INTERNATIONAL MONETARY REFORM

1. John P. Judd and Glenn D. Rudebusch, "Taylor's Rule and the Fed: 1970–1997," *FRBSF Economic Review* 1998, no. 3; and Richard Clarida, Jordi Gali, and Mark Gertler, "Monetary Policy Rules and Macroeconomic Stability: Evidence and Some Theory," *Quarterly Journal of Economics* 115, no. 1 (February 2000): 147–180.

2. Stephen G. Cecchetti, Peter Hooper, Bruce C. Kasman, Kermit L. Schoenholtz, and Mark W. Watson, "Understanding the Evolving Inflation Process," presented at the US Monetary Policy Forum, March 9, 2007, Washington, DC.

3. In my view, QE had little if any positive impact. See Johannes C. Stroebel and John B. Taylor, "Estimated Impact of the Federal Reserve's Mortgage-Backed Securities Purchase Program," *International Journal of Central Banking* 8, no. 2 (June 2012): 1–42.

4. See Rudiger Ahrend, "Monetary Ease: A Factor Behind Financial Crises? Some Evidence from OECD Countries," *Economics: The Open-Access, Open-Assessment E-Journal* 4, 2010-12 (April 14, 2010); and Boris Hofmann and Bilyana Bogdanova, "Taylor Rules and Monetary Policy: A Global Great Deviation?" *BIS Quarterly Review*, September 2012.

5. Richard Clarida, "Discussion of 'The Federal Reserve in a Globalized World Economy,'" conference on "The Federal Reserve's Role in the Global Economy: A Historical Perspective," Dallas Federal Reserve Bank, September 2014.

6. Alex Nikolsko-Rzhevskyy, David H. Papell, and Ruxandra Prodan, "Deviations from Rules-Based Policy and Their Effects," *Journal of Economic Dynamics and Control* 49 (December 2014).

7. See their commentary in the conference proceedings also published in the *Journal of Economic Dynamics and Control* 49 (December 2014).

8. John B. Taylor, "Legislating a Rule for Monetary Policy," *The Cato Journal* 31, no. 3 (2011): 407–415.

9. Hearings on March 3, 2015, Before the Committee on Banking, Housing, and Urban Affairs, United States Senate.

10. See Carl E. Walsh, "Goals and Rules in Central Bank Design," and Alex Nikolsko-Rzhevskyy, David Papell, and Ruxandra Prodan, "Policy Rule Legislation in Practice," in *Central Bank Governance and Oversight Reform*, John H. Cochrane and John B. Taylor, eds. (Stanford, CA: Hoover Institution Press, 2016).

11. "Monetary Policy and the State of the Economy," hearings on February 25, 2015, Before the House Financial Services Committee.

12. For example, John B. Taylor, *Macroeconomic Policy in a World Economy: From Econometric Design to Practical Operation* (New York: W. W. Norton, 1993).

13. Transcript published in the *Journal of Policy Modeling* 36, no. 4 (2013).

14. Atul Gawande, "The Checklist: If Something So Simple Can Transform Intensive Care, What Else Can It Do?" *The New Yorker*, December 10, 2007.

15. Ben S. Bernanke, "'Constrained Discretion' and Monetary Policy," remarks before the Money Marketeers of New York University, February 3, 2003.

16. Contrast the IMF's "The Liberalization and Management of Capital Flows: An Institutional View," November 14, 2012, which states that "capital flow management measures [that is, capital controls] can be useful," with the IMF's "Communiqué of the Interim Committee of the Board of Governors of the International Monetary Fund," news release 97/44, September 21, 1997, which called for "an amendment of the Fund's Articles" to promote "an orderly liberalization of capital movements."

17. Milton Friedman, *Capitalism and Freedom* (Chicago: University of Chicago Press, 1962), 51.

18. These are goals articulated by Paul Volcker in his "Remarks" at the Bretton Woods Committee Annual Meeting, May 21, 2014.

CHAPTER 7: A BLUEPRINT FOR EFFECTIVE FINANCIAL REFORM

1. Many issues in this essay are treated in more depth in John H. Cochrane, "Toward a Run-Free Financial System," in *Across the Great Divide: New Perspectives on the Financial Crisis,* Martin Neil Baily and John B. Taylor, eds., 197–249 (Stanford, CA: Hoover Institution Press, 2014).

2. This debt is explained in detail in John Cochrane, "A New Structure for U.S. Federal Debt," in *The $13 Trillion Question: Managing the U.S. Government Debt*, ed. David Wessel, 91–146 (Washington, DC: Brookings Institution Press, 2015).

CHAPTER 8: EDUCATION AND THE NATION'S FUTURE

1. The figure reports the separate influence of aggregate test scores for nations on real annual growth in GDP per capita between 1960 and 2000. Underlying this is a regression analysis that also includes the initial GDP per capita in 1960, reflecting the fact that nations starting behind can grow faster because they just have to imitate what is done elsewhere instead of inventing new things. For details, see Hanushek and Woessmann (2015).

2. The details of these projections can be found in Hanushek, Peterson, and Woessmann (2013) and Hanushek and Woessmann (2015). The gains are calculated as the difference between projected GDP based on current labor force quality and improved quality through better schooling. Real GDP at current quality is projected to grow at 1.5 percent per year.

3. These calculations use estimates of the variation in teacher quality from existing value-added studies and from labor market studies of the value of added achievement to project added earnings for teachers at different quality levels (see Hanushek (2011)). The estimates for different size classes assume that added students over the range of the projections have no impact on class achievement. This assumption is controversial; see Krueger (1999) and Hanushek (2003). Class size or students taught refers to full-time equivalents for teachers with multiple classes of students.

4. As is well-known, families also exert a strong force on child learning, but the discussion here focuses on schools, because that is where policy has greatest leverage and legitimacy. Since the emphasis on families in the Coleman Report in 1966, some have discounted schools, but current research makes it clear that schools and teachers have large potential impacts. See Coleman et al. (1966) and the re-evaluation in Hanushek (2016).

5. The Washington, DC, system increases the base pay for the best teachers while firing the least effective, thus changing the career pay according to performance. See the evaluation by Dee and Wyckoff (2015). See also Figlio and Kenny (2007).

6. Atkinson et al. (2009), Lavy (2009), Muralidharan and Sundararaman (2011), Woessmann (2011).

7. See changes in state policies in National Council on Teacher Quality (2015).

8. An appellate court overturned this ruling in 2016, and final judgment

has yet to be reached. But even this appellate court indicated that existing tenure and dismissal laws were harming California students.

9. Carnoy and Loeb (2002), Hanushek and Raymond (2005), Figlio and Loeb (2011).

10. Figlio and Rouse (2006).

11. See, for example, Bishop (1995, 1997) and Woessmann et al. (2009). The college entry examinations in the United States do provide external exit examinations on a voluntary basis, but no research exists about potential impacts on the K-12 schools.

12. CREDO (2013).

REFERENCES FOR CHAPTER 8

Atkinson, Adele, Simon Burgess, Bronwyn Croxson, Paul Gregg, Carol Propper, Helen Slater, and Deborah Wilson. 2009. "Evaluating the impact of performance-related pay for teachers in England." *Labour Economics* 16, no. 3: 251–261.

Bishop, John H. 1995. "The impact of curriculum-based external examinations on school priorities and student learning." *International Journal of Educational Research* 23, no. 8: 653–752.

Bishop, John H. 1997. "The effect of national standards and curriculum-based examinations on achievement." *American Economic Review* 87, no. 2: 260–264.

Carnoy, Martin, and Susanna Loeb. 2002. "Does external accountability affect student outcomes? A cross-state analysis." *Educational Evaluation and Policy Analysis* 24, no. 4 (Winter): 305–331.

Coleman, James S., Ernest Q. Campbell, Carol J. Hobson, James McPartland, Alexander M. Mood, Frederic D. Weinfeld, and Robert L. York. 1966. *Equality of educational opportunity*. Washington, D.C.: U.S. Government Printing Office.

CREDO. 2013. *National charter school study 2013*. Stanford, CA: Center for Research on Education Outcomes, Stanford University.

Dee, Thomas S., and James Wyckoff. 2015. "Incentives, selection, and teacher performance: Evidence from IMPACT." *Journal of Policy Analysis and Management* 34, no. 2 (Spring): 267–297.

Figlio, David, and Susanna Loeb. 2011. "School accountability." In *Handbook of the Economics of Education, Vol. 3*, edited by Eric A. Hanushek, Stephen Machin, and Ludger Woessmann. Amsterdam: North Holland: 383–421.

Figlio, David N., and Lawrence W. Kenny. 2007. "Individual teacher incentives and student performance." *Journal of Public Economics* 91, no. 5–6 (June): 901–914.

Figlio, David N., and Cecilia Elena Rouse. 2006. "Do accountability and voucher threats improve low-performing schools?" *Journal of Public Economics* 90, no. 1–2 (January): 239–255.

Hanushek, Eric A. 2003. "The failure of input-based schooling policies." *Economic Journal* 113, no. 485 (February): F64–F98.

Hanushek, Eric A. 2011. "The economic value of higher teacher quality." *Economics of Education Review* 30, no. 3 (June): 466–479.

Hanushek, Eric A. 2016. "What Matters for Achievement: Updating Coleman on the Influence of Families and Schools." *Education Next* 16, no. 2 (Spring): 22–30.

Hanushek, Eric A., Paul E. Peterson, and Ludger Woessmann. 2013. *Endangering prosperity: A global view of the American school.* Washington, DC: Brookings Institution Press.

Hanushek, Eric A., and Margaret E. Raymond. 2005. "Does school accountability lead to improved student performance?" *Journal of Policy Analysis and Management* 24, no. 2 (Spring): 297–327.

Hanushek, Eric A., and Ludger Woessmann. 2015. *The knowledge capital of nations: Education and the economics of growth.* Cambridge, MA: MIT Press.

Krueger, Alan B. 1999. "Experimental estimates of education production functions." *Quarterly Journal of Economics* 114, no. 2 (May): 497–532.

Lavy, Victor. 2009. "Performance pay and teachers' effort, productivity, and grading ethics." *American Economic Review* 99, no. 5 (December): 1979–2011.

Muralidharan, Karthik, and Venkatesh Sundararaman. 2011. "Teacher performance pay: Experimental evidence from India." *Journal of Political Economy* 119, no. 1 (February): 39–77.

National Council on Teacher Quality. 2015. *State teacher policy yearbook, 2015.* Washington: National Council on Teacher Quality.

OECD. 2010. PISA 2009 results: What students know and can do—Student performance in mathematics, reading and science (Volume I). Paris: Organisation for Economic Co-operation and Development.

OECD. 2013. PISA 2012 results: What students know and can do—Student performance in mathematics, reading and science (Volume I). Paris: Organisation for Economic Co-operation and Development.

Woessmann, Ludger. 2011. "Cross-country evidence on teacher performance pay." *Economics of Education Review* 30, no. 3 (June): 404–418.

Woessmann, Ludger, Elke Luedemann, Gabriela Schuetz, and Martin R. West. 2009. *School accountability, autonomy, and choice around the world.* Cheltenham, UK: Edward Elgar.

IN BRIEF: A WORLD AWASH IN CHANGE

1. Martin Wight, *Power Politics* (London: Royal Institute of International Affairs, 1979), 148.

2. L. G. Mitchell and William B. Todd, eds., *The Writings and Speeches of Edmund Burke, Vol. 8: The French Revolution: 1790-1794* (Oxford: Oxford University Press, 1988), 391. See also, Edmund Burke, *Three Memorials on French Affairs Written in the Years 1791, 1792 and 1793* (London: F. & C. Rivington, 1797).

CHAPTER 12: DIPLOMACY IN A TIME OF TRANSITION

1. Norman Angell, *The Great Illusion* (London: William Heinemann, 1912).

2. Herbert Hoover, *Foreign Affairs: A Report to the Congress, February 1949* (Washington, DC: US Government Printing Office, 1949).

3. Harry S. Truman Library & Museum, *Public Papers of the Presidents*, no. 47, "Special Message to the Congress on Reorganization of the State Department."

4. Courtesy of Ford Cooper, retired Foreign Service officer. See also the report, "American Diplomacy at Risk," American Academy of Diplomacy, April 1, 2015; and Dennis C. Jett, *American Ambassadors: The Past, Present, and Future of America's Diplomats* (New York: Palgrave Macmillan, 2014), 50.

5. For further discussions of these two forms of diplomacy, see James Goodby, "Diplomatic Cathedral-Building," *The Foreign Service Journal*, September 2002: 71; and James Goodby, "The Putin Doctrine and Preventive Diplomacy," *The Foreign Service Journal*, November 2014: 22.

6. Boutros Boutros-Ghali, "Agenda for Peace," Report of the Secretary General, United Nations, June 17, 1992.

7. "American Diplomacy at Risk."

8. Alexander George, *Bridging the Gap: Theory and Practice in Foreign Policy* (Washington, DC: US Institute of Peace Press, 1993).

9. Charles King, "The Decline of International Studies: Why Flying Blind Is Dangerous," *Foreign Affairs*, July/August 2015: 88–98.

10. Ibid., 90.

11. Jon Davies, "The Diplomatic Academy; A First for Britain's Foreign Office," *The Foreign Service Journal*, July/August 2015: 37–40.

12. Ibid., 39.

13. Thomas A. Shannon Jr., "The Long Diplomacy: How a Changing World Creates New Opportunities for Partnership between Scholars and Practitioners," in *Scholars, Policymakers, & International Affairs; Finding Common Cause*, chap. 11, eds. A. F. Lowenthal & Mariano E. Bertucci (Baltimore: Johns Hopkins University Press, 2014).

CONTRIBUTORS

SCOTT W. ATLAS, MD, is the David and Joan Traitel Senior Fellow at Stanford University's Hoover Institution and a member of the Hoover Institution's Working Group on Health Care Policy. He investigates the impact of government and the private sector on access, quality, pricing, and innovation in health care, and he is a frequent policy adviser to government leaders in those areas. Dr. Atlas's most recent book is *Restoring Quality Health Care: A Six Point Plan for Comprehensive Reform at Lower Cost* (Hoover Institution Press, 2016). As professor and chief of neuroradiology at Stanford University Medical Center from 1998 until 2012 and during his prior academic positions, Dr. Atlas trained more than one hundred neuroradiology fellows, many of whom are now leaders in the field throughout the world. Dr. Atlas received a BS degree in biology from the University of Illinois in Urbana-Champaign and an MD degree from the University of Chicago School of Medicine.

MICHAEL J. BOSKIN is a senior fellow at the Hoover Institution and the T. M. Friedman Professor of Economics at Stanford University. He is also a research associate at the National Bureau of Economic Research and advises governments and businesses globally. Boskin served as chairman of the President's Council of Economic Advisers (CEA) from 1989 to 1993. He chaired the blue-ribbon Commission on Consumer Price Index, whose report has transformed the way government statistical agencies around the world measure inflation, GDP, and productivity. He is internationally recognized for his research on world economic growth, tax and budget theory and policy, US saving and consumption patterns, and the implications of changing technology and demography on capital, labor, and product markets, subjects about which he has authored more than one hundred fifty books and articles. Boskin received his BA with highest honors in 1967 from the University of California, Berkeley, where he also received his MA and PhD.

JOHN H. COCHRANE is a senior fellow at the Hoover Institution and a research associate of the National Bureau of Economic Research. Before joining Hoover, Cochrane was a professor of finance at the University of Chicago's Booth School of Business, and earlier at its Economics Department. Cochrane's recent publications include the book *Asset Pricing* and articles on dynamics in stock and bond markets, the volatility of exchange rates, the term structure of interest rates, the returns to venture capital, liquidity premiums in stock prices, the relation between stock prices and business cycles, and option pricing when investors can't perfectly hedge. He was a junior staff economist on the Council of Economic Advisers (1982–83). He also maintains the *Grumpy Economist* blog. Cochrane earned a bachelor's degree in physics at MIT and his PhD in economics at the University of California, Berkeley.

JOHN F. COGAN is the Leonard and Shirley Ely Senior Fellow at the Hoover Institution and a faculty member in the Public Policy Program at Stanford University. Cogan is an expert in domestic policy. His current research is focused on US budget and fiscal policy, federal entitlement programs, and health care, and he has published widely in professional journals in both economics and political science. He served as assistant secretary for policy in the

US Department of Labor from 1981 to 1983. He was later associate director in the Office of Management and Budget (OMB) and was appointed deputy director in 1988. Cogan has since served on numerous congressional, presidential, and California state advisory commissions. He received his AB in 1969 and his PhD in 1976 from the University of California at Los Angeles, both in economics.

ADMIRAL JAMES O. ELLIS JR. is the Annenberg Distinguished Fellow at the Hoover Institution. In 2012 he retired as president and chief executive officer of the Institute of Nuclear Power Operations (INPO). Admiral Ellis earlier completed a distinguished thirty-nine-year Navy career as commander of the United States Strategic Command. In this role, he was responsible for the global command and control of United States strategic and space forces, reporting directly to the secretary of defense. He earlier commanded the nuclear-powered aircraft carrier USS *Abraham Lincoln* and in 1996 served as a carrier battle group commander in the Taiwan Straits crisis, following selection to rear admiral. Senior shore assignments included commander in chief, US Naval Forces, Europe, and commander in chief, Allied Forces, Southern Europe. A 1969 graduate of the US Naval Academy, Ellis holds a master's degree in aerospace engineering from Georgia Tech, served multiple tours as a Navy fighter pilot, and is a graduate of the Navy Test Pilot School and the Navy Fighter Weapons School (Top Gun). Ellis was recently elected to the National Academy of Engineering.

JAMES E. GOODBY is an Annenberg Distinguished Visiting Fellow at the Hoover Institution. He has served in the US Foreign Service, achieving the rank of career minister, and was appointed to five ambassadorial-rank positions by Presidents Carter, Reagan, and Clinton, including ambassador to Finland. During his Foreign Service career he was involved as a negotiator or as a policy adviser in the creation of the International Atomic Energy Agency, the negotiation of the limited nuclear test ban treaty, START, the Conference on Disarmament in Europe, and cooperative threat reduction (the Nunn-Lugar program). He has authored extensively on these subjects. Goodby taught at Georgetown, Syracuse, and Carnegie Mellon universities and is Distinguished Service Professor Emeritus at Carnegie Mellon. Awards include the Presidential Distinguished Service Award, the State Department's Superior and Distinguished Honor Awards, the Commander's Cross of the Order of Merit of Germany, and the inaugural Heinz Award in Public Policy.

ERIC A. HANUSHEK is the Paul and Jean Hanna Senior Fellow at Stanford University's Hoover Institution. A leader in the development of the economic analysis of educational issues, his research spans the impact on achievement of teacher quality, high-stakes accountability, and class-size reduction. He pioneered measuring teacher quality on the basis of student achievement, the foundation for current research into the value-added evaluations of teachers and schools. His latest book is *The Knowledge Capital of Nations: Education and the Economics of Growth*. Hanushek previously held academic appointments at the University of Rochester, Yale University, and the US Air Force Academy and served in government as deputy director of the Congressional Budget Office. He was awarded the Fordham Prize for Distinguished Scholarship in 2004. A distinguished graduate of the United States Air Force Academy, he completed his PhD in economics at the Massachusetts Institute of Technology.

GENERAL JAMES N. MATTIS, the Davies Family Distinguished Visiting Fellow at the Hoover Institution, is an expert on national security issues, especially strategy, innovation, the effective use of military force, and the Middle East. He heads a project on the gap between civil and military perspectives and is writing a book on leadership. Before coming to Hoover, Mattis was the commander of the US Central Command (CENTCOM). While commanding CENTCOM from 2010 to 2013, he was responsible for military operations involving more than 200,000 US soldiers, sailors, airmen, Coast Guardsmen, and Marines in Afghanistan, Iraq, and eighteen other countries in the Middle East and south-central Asia. General Mattis commanded at multiple levels in his forty-two-year career as a Marine, including serving as NATO's Supreme Allied Commander for Transformation and commander of the United States Joint Forces Command (USJFCOM). He graduated from Central Washington State University in 1972. He is also a graduate of the Amphibious Warfare School, Marine Corps Command and Staff College, and the National War College.

KORI SCHAKE is a research fellow at the Hoover Institution. She was senior policy adviser to the 2008 McCain-Palin campaign, responsible for policy development and outreach in the areas of foreign and defense policy. Earlier, she was the deputy director for policy planning in the State Department. In addition to staff management, she worked on resourcing and organizational effectiveness issues, including a study of what it would take to "transform" the State Department so as to enable integrated political, economic, and military strategies. During President George W. Bush's first term, she was the director for defense strategy and requirements on the National Security Council. She was responsible for interagency coordination for long-term defense planning and coalition maintenance issues. She has held the Distinguished Chair of International Security Studies at West Point, and also served in the faculties of the Johns Hopkins School of Advanced International Studies, the University of Maryland's School of Public Affairs, and the National Defense University.

GEORGE PRATT SHULTZ is the Thomas W. and Susan B. Ford Distinguished Fellow at the Hoover Institution. He has had a distinguished career in government, in academia, and in the world of business. He is one of two individuals who have held four different federal cabinet posts; he has taught at three of this country's great universities; and for eight years he was president of a major engineering and construction company. Shultz was sworn in July 16, 1982, as the sixtieth US secretary of state and served until January 20, 1989. He attended Princeton University, graduating with a BA in economics, whereupon he enlisted in the US Marine Corps, serving through 1945. He later earned a PhD in industrial economics from the Massachusetts Institute of Technology. In 1989, Shultz was awarded the Medal of Freedom, the nation's highest civilian honor. His most recent book is *Issues on My Mind: Strategies for the Future* (Hoover Institution Press, 2013).

JOHN B. TAYLOR is the George P. Shultz Senior Fellow in Economics at the Hoover Institution and the Mary and Robert Raymond Professor of Economics at Stanford University. He chairs the Hoover Working Group on Economic Policy and is director of Stanford's Introductory Economics Center. Taylor's fields of expertise are monetary policy, fiscal policy, and international economics, subjects about which he has widely authored both policy and academic texts. Taylor served as senior economist on President Ford's and President Carter's Council of Economic Advisers, as a member of President George H. W. Bush's Council of Economic Advisers, and as a senior economic adviser to numerous presidential campaigns. He was a member of the Congressional Budget Office's Panel of Economic Advisers, and from 2001 to 2005 he served as undersecretary of the treasury for international affairs. Taylor received a BA in economics summa cum laude from Princeton University in 1968 and a PhD in economics from Stanford University in 1973.

INDEX